D1277287

*Mindfulness*
at Work

# Mindfulness at Work

*Flourishing in the Workplace*

**Maria Arpa**

*Leaping Hare Press*

This paperback edition published in the UK in 2019 by
*Leaping Hare Press*
An imprint of The Quarto Group
The Old Brewery, 6 Blundell Street
London N7 9BH, United Kingdom
**T** (0)20 7700 6700
www.QuartoKnows.com

First published in hardback in 2013

British Library Cataloguing-in-Publication Data
A catalogue record for this book is available from the British Library

ISBN: 978-1-78240-934-2

This book was conceived, designed and produced by
*Leaping Hare Press*

58 West Street, Brighton BN1 2RA, United Kingdom

Creative Director  PETER BRIDGEWATER
Publisher  SUSAN KELLEY
Commissioning Editor  MONICA PERDONI
Editorial Director  TOM KITCH
Art Director  JAMES LAWRENCE
Designer  GINNY ZEAL
Illustrators  MELVYN EVANS

Printed in China

1 3 5 7 9 10 8 6 4 2

# CONTENTS

# INTRODUCTION

*Most of us believe we have no choice but to work
and many people have little choice about what
work they do. Education, wealth and environment
can dictate the options available — yet we have all
heard of people who are 'self-made', who rejected the
limitations and broke through the barriers. But finding
fulfilment at work doesn't always require a drastic
change; sometimes addressing conflicts and
relationships in the workplace can make all the
difference. This book is filled with exercises, meditations
and a personal two-week plan so you can learn to be
mindful about work.*

## WORKING WITHOUT FULFILMENT

◆

*In an ideal world, your work would be a source of fulfilment, provid-ing you with meaning and purpose. Too often, though, this isn't the case. When the world around you isn't performing how you would like, your choices are either a change of attitude or a change of di-rection. Mindfulness will help you choose.*

MY SON, SAM, IS HOME FROM UNIVERSITY and hoping to find work for the summer. It's tough. Unemployment is high right now. In his words, 'I'm determined to find a job or I'll end up spending the whole summer on the PlayStation.' His first priority is to earn some cash; but that's not all of it. He wants to do something meaningful, which is not always possible because it depends on what work is available. This creates a dilemma for many young people at the start of their working lives – whether to take any job to earn money, even if the work is joyless or meaningless, or to hold out for mean-ing and purpose, even if it means being broke. This choice, which most of us have faced, can set a blueprint for how our working life will turn out. Many take whatever work they can get and while they are grateful for having employment, the workplace is a source of a great deal of unhappiness.

While pondering this, I came across the latest Happiness at Work Index findings that stated that one out of four people in the UK is unhappy at work. Even if this is an exaggeration, something must be wrong with our workplaces if even 10 per cent of the workforce is unhappy. For that much unhappiness to exist, we *must* be telling ourselves that we are powerless to change things. I know I thought that once upon a time. Many reasons were given for dissatisfaction – including poor management, low pay and lack of opportunity – but 48 per cent of respondents said their job held no significant meaning for them. Clearly there is a problem that needs confronting.

**So What Can Be Done?**

If you are one of the many people who are dissatisfied with their lot at work and feel powerless to change it, this book is for you. If you can understand what it is that drives your unhappiness at work, you can address it and plan for change. If you see yourself as powerless, then you *are* powerless – but that doesn't mean you have to *remain* powerless. Spending many hours a day with a group of people you didn't choose to share this much of your life with, in a job you are not satisfied with, will create a pressure cooker of tension. Left unresolved, it will fester under the surface, creating stress and taking its toll on your emotional and physical well-being.

However, by using the mindfulness techniques explained in the book, you can reduce stress, develop contentment, influence your working environment and make better choices. My aim is to share what I have learned through my passionate desire to turn work into productive play.

## WHAT IS MINDFULNESS?

*For the purposes of this book, I define mindfulness as a conscious awareness of the present moment and recognition of what is really happening. This requires us to observe rather than judge events — which is easier said than done, because we are usually unaware of the lens through which we are examining the world.*

T HAT LENS OFTEN DISTORTS REALITY in order to substantiate the beliefs we hold. Mindfulness is a 'waking up' process. It asks us to live consciously, to have regard for our sensations, feelings, thoughts and actions. A significant part of mindfulness is meditation. This allows you to become aware of yourself in the present. We learn meditation by focusing on our breathing; try spending thirty seconds right now focusing on your breathing and just slow it down a little. Mindfulness brings empowerment and self-responsibility and this leads to better self-care, decision making and participation in life. At work, it requires us to constantly review our individual and collective contribution and the results of those contributions.

### Looking Back

Because congruity between what I say and what I do matters to me, I found myself looking back on choices I have made. I have thrived in some settings and walked out of others. In all cases I have reflected upon and learned from the experiences.

One of my more miserable recollections was a boss who, on a daily basis and without any provocation, would shout angrily across the office to the whole staff: 'Remember, if you don't like it here, there are plenty of people waiting in the wings to take your place.' He believed that the fear of losing one's job was motivational.

What is extraordinary is that he had a dream team in place who would work all night to meet a deadline. Individually, they could each find work anywhere and probably for more money, but I had deliberately recruited a team who liked each other and could work cooperatively. This made work enjoyable for them and everyone agreed that having fun at work was more important than earning more money. What I didn't anticipate was an owner who failed to recognise that his team would be prepared to make more money for him in return for a fun atmosphere; instead he found their camaraderie a threat.

The work was of a very high standard, all the clients were happy and profits were good. But the owner's capacity to trust was so limited, he used to count the stamps to see if any had been stolen. He was completely unable to enjoy the good times. Sometimes people can't. Over time, the atmosphere deteriorated. After all the work I had put in to create a motivated team, I just felt powerless, frustrated and resentful.

One day I walked out. I decided to change it all and start my own business, vowing to enjoy work above all else. So at the age of twenty-eight I began a challenging journey.

## Life in the Fast Lane

The business I set up was an advertising agency. It made money and employed people and we definitely appreciated the good times. I defined myself through my work. I saw myself as a 'businesswoman', and as I started to hang out with other successful businesswomen, we saw ourselves as women 'breaking through the glass ceiling'. I became more and more formidable, in line with the role I was attributing to myself. I was also bringing up my two children and coping with a floundering marriage, but I was a businesswoman first. I enjoyed being a mother but somehow I couldn't allow myself the time to truly enjoy being a parent.

Then something snapped. I found myself calling the nanny to arrange a breakfast meeting with the children, then aged four and five, and I realized something was drastically wrong. That moment of realization may have been my first experience of mindfulness, though I wouldn't have recognized it at the time. It was a moment of awareness where I was able to observe my life from a distance and question it without judgement or blame. I asked myself, 'Is this really what I want for myself?' The question was too big, because on some level I knew that answering it would change everything. I was scared. I remember saying at the time, 'Every time I contemplate answering that question, it feels like I'm about to jump out of a plane with no parachute.' I was the wrong side of thirty-five and hovered on that question for a couple of years.

## The Moment of Truth

One day I confronted the question: '*What do I really want for myself?*' The answer was clear: I wanted to feel more joy in my work. It was also clear that although I was meeting my needs for success and fulfilment, I wasn't feeling much joy – because the truth was that being a 'formidable businesswoman' with a reputation was no fun. My ego loved it but my soul was screaming out for me to stop. I realized that change was upon me. Life in its present form was no longer tolerable.

It was a struggle to give up a materially wealthy lifestyle to try something new. In those moments of mindfulness, I reminded myself that I was paying too high a price for what the world judged as success but I was increasingly experiencing as a spiritual desert. I had developed a high level of robustness to get me through the rigours of work, but it left me insensitive to the important stuff such as spending time playing with my children and enjoying nature. I decided that, however the change manifested, my work would be a part of who I am rather than an external role, and that people would come first. I became compelled to find out whether I could sustain myself and my family on that basis. What a risk. What a journey. There was no going back.

**Q** *Did it work?*   **A** Mostly.

**Q** *Has it been easy?*   **A** No.

**Q** *Do I have more joy in my life?*   **A** Absolutely yes.

## Taking the Plunge

I took a risk. I knew I didn't want to work on anything directly to do with consumerism. What I did want was more control over my time, more authentic communication with people, development of my intuitive and creative skills and a sense of contribution. I decided to become a counsellor and reiki master. Following more research and career progression, I also became a mediator and expert in conflict resolution. I have two channels for this work – my own private practice and a charity, which I founded to ensure that my work can reach people who don't have the financial means to access it.

Now I'm in my fifties, and while I will probably never stop contributing in some way, I am also considering a time when I might not devote so many hours to work. I'm thinking about how much time I have to complete the contribution I really want to make, which is sharing what I know about conflict and how to resolve it. Conflict is everywhere – it is a part of life, and most of it is inside us. I hope I can make the journey easier for others than it was for me. Welcome to this book!

## A Sense of Community

While working through this book, remember that any workplace with more than one person in it is a community. A community is a group of people helping each other. Helping each other can be very rewarding and fulfilling; it can also be full of conflict and competition. In order to reduce the tension, all communities need some way of coming together and bonding. While I don't subscribe to any organized religion, I know that most faith groups have some form of group contemplation built into their practices, which is a very useful way of bringing people together and creating community. This is something most profit-driven workplaces lack, but we don't have to wait for others to create community for us; there is nothing stopping us from creating those conditions with our colleagues and peers.

This book will show you how to evaluate your own situation and how to improve your relationships with your colleagues. It contains a series of exercises, which you can work through in your own time; everything is designed to fit into your 'day-to-day'. Read through the book, then return and plan how you will make use of the exercises. If you are new to mindfulness and meditation but committed to making the time to work through this book, I estimate you will need about twelve weeks to complete it while carrying on with your day-to-day. The chapters are set out as pieces of a jigsaw. Each chapter introduces a different theme for you to reflect on and the whole programme comes together in Chapter Five, where you begin to examine your options by understanding your motivations. Finally, in Chapter Six, you can make informed decisions and see them through. My hope is that, by the end of the book, you'll be well on your way to finding more joy in your working life.

# CHAPTER ONE

# WAKE UP
# & SMELL THE
# COFFEE

*Welcome to the beginning of the journey.*
*In this chapter we will try to understand how so*
*many of us came to be unhappy at work. My starting*
*point is what we were shown at school, where teachers*
*modelled how to act in a workplace. We unconsciously*
*accepted this as 'the way it is' and our unique and*
*individual experience of this has generated our*
*behaviours and responses. By remembering and*
*acknowledging those experiences, you will*
*understand their effect on the choices you*
*have made about work and can begin*
*to take steps to remedy this.*

## IDENTIFYING YOUR GOAL

◆

*In my role as a counsellor and mediator, a client may tell me that they want to address the problem of their unhappiness at work. One of the first questions I ask is this: 'Are you here because you want to find peace with yourself so you can continue on your current path or because you want to find the strength to make a change?'*

ASK YOURSELF: do you want to stay put and find joy in the status quo or move on and find a different source of joy? While the direction you choose will partially depend on your circumstances, resources and support network, it will also depend on your attitude and beliefs in relation to what you are capable of and what you are worth. Your current circumstances and resources are the consequences of the choices you made in the past based on your beliefs and attitudes to the situations you were facing. What we want to do in this book is consciously gather information and evidence about your past choices and the environment you were exposed to so that you can make the best possible decisions in the future.

### 'I'm not asking for much'

A friend was complaining to me about her work. She ended by saying, 'It's not as if I'm asking for much.' I thought about this, and my reply was, 'Yes, you're not asking for much, and that is exactly what the Universe has provided – not much.'

Many people are settling for less happiness than they want for themselves and are discontented. This is a social norm. We were conditioned to be discontented because the pursuit of economic growth means we always want more – even if we get into debt to achieve it. Debt-driven growth hurts us psychologically and socially rather than enriches us.

This discontent can be challenged in two ways. Either we can find a way to see the abundance in what we already have or we can create a different path to abundance.

I'm going to explore some of the ways in which we have set ourselves up for misery and suffering and how this plays out in the workplace. Our blind acceptance of the status quo, as learned from our early experiences of teachers and other leaders, is a primary source of unhappiness. You may find some of my writing will arouse feelings in you, but it won't cause them, it simply triggers them, and understanding them can make you aware of how you interpret the world.

As you read the book, try not to agree or disagree with my propositions. Instead, just allow them. By allowing, you will experience emergence.

---

'And the day came when the risk to remain tight in a
bud was more painful than the risk it took to blossom.'

ANAÏS NIN (1903–77)
AUTHOR & DIARIST

---

## Emergence

Emergence contradicts conventional Western processes for change as a top-down, strategic plan mandated by a hierarchy. Emergence is the outcome of *allowing* rather than *controlling*. I'm currently part of a team working on a Forgiveness conference. As a group we were grappling with the theme and the plan, but over dinner the group exchanged thoughts and reflections and the collective knowledge grew. By having an open mind, a theme and plan emerged.

Now apply this to your own change process. If you keep changing job in response to discomfort in order to try to find a workplace you like, you don't have an open mind. You are attached to one way of answering a problem. If you were to observe, reflect and review circumstances, environment, beliefs and attitudes, a more sustainable plan will emerge.

If you find some parts of this book difficult to access, you are encountering your resistance. It pops up for all of us in varying degrees at different times, according to the stimulus we encounter. Doing nothing about a situation is also a form of resistance, though a form of which we are less aware.

## Overcoming Resistance

To embrace change, within the workplace or outside it, we first have to overcome resistance. This means recognizing what we are defending and imagining what it would be like to 'let go' of defending. To do this, we have to experiment.

## TRY THIS

Pick up any small object that is to hand such as a pen. Concentrate on the object. Handle it and look at it from all angles without commenting and without using words to think about it. Just allow the object to exist. Do this for a minute if you can. Could you do this for a whole minute without any discomfort? Did you 'allow' it, without having any words? What emerges about yourself as a result of the exercise?

Life can be seen as a series of experiments where you try something, review it, learn from it, and then try something slightly different. The more experiments you make, the more you can start to see the gap between reality and what you tell yourself. You can start with low-risk experiments just to find out how it feels to do something different. For example, if you believe yourself to be shy, initiate a conversation with a colleague you know by sight but haven't spoken to. Use your discretion – I wouldn't try this in a situation where my intentions could be misinterpreted. The conversation's outcome isn't important; you are interested in how it feels and what resources it will need from you to do it differently. A review of the process – from your decision about *what* to try to actually trying it – will enable you to gauge your resistance level.

## DISCONTENTMENT AT WORK

◆

*If you want more happiness at work, if you want to develop self-confidence and healthy relationships with others in the workplace, you first have to learn that competition, rivalry, expectations and rules do not generate happiness, self-confidence or healthy relationships. In fact, they perpetuate discontentment.*

COMPETITION INVOLVES WINNING – and when you choose to measure your self-worth through winning, you are attaching it to external validation. The same applies to rivalry, where success is measured by triumphing over others. It causes mistrust, fear and divisiveness between individuals or teams, not sound working relationships. Rules and expectations have a similar effect. The supposition is that we need external pressure to motivate us to work, but we are less likely to find happiness if our motivations are derived from external sources rather than our personal desire to flourish.

### Competition & Rivalry

The first and most important lesson that creates discontent is the belief that competition and rivalry are healthy. Early experiences at school instilled in us a belief that competition is the way to success, and that competition is only a problem if we become obsessive about winning. By accepting competition as 'natural', we do not examine or question it.

There have been many studies on Competitive State Anxiety, which indicate that competition increases anxiety and reduces our powers of concentration. It limits our ability to share with colleagues since rivals will not want to increase others' learning or give others an advantage in the eyes of the boss. It promotes other people as obstacles to our own success. Once engaged in competition, some people just become expert at winning, whatever the cost. This can become an organizational problem that spreads like a virus.

*Nature or Nurture?*

Throughout history, children have been encouraged to play competitive games; we teach children that this is entertainment, but the reality is that some children dread those games. I have observed that children left to their own devices will more often than not opt for collaborative games.

We compare children with each other by giving them marks at school so that they compete for a grade, even if that means learning things parrot-fashion rather than enjoying the learning. When my daughter set out to achieve a high mark in her International Baccalaureate, she realized that she could cram information to pass the exam to compete for a place at university. Afterwards she immediately forgot it because it was of no actual use to her. She was competing for a grade and neither of us could see any internal benefit to her well-being in doing so.

We introduce children to the hierarchical institution that is school without adequate preparation for understanding a structure that trades on the practice of competitive communication and insists that being right and winning is the best way to live, when it's actually stressful and likely to escalate conflict between people.

Alfie Kohn is an authority on human behaviour, education and parenting, whose case against competition has been widely debated. He believes that 'trying to be number one and trying to do a task well are two different things'. It's important to understand that using force to get a child to do something is competing with them for power.

Of course, the reality is that competition exists in our systems and we need to learn about it. But learning about something doesn't mean we have to participate in it. We can recognize it exists and then mindfully consider how we wish to engage in a competitive workplace. We can seek to explore the true value of our contribution to the workplace and not rate our success on how we stand up against our colleagues.

### Expectations

Living up to the expectations of others is another source of discontent and we have all been guilty of it. When you let other people set the standards for your success and it isn't congruent with how you feel or what you want, you will become unhappy. Parents have a large part to play in setting

the example for this through having high expectations for their children. What most parents really want is for their children to be happy and content but the problems arise when they define what that happiness should be and how their children should attain it. Once we buy into this as a way of pleasing others to keep the peace, you can be fairly sure that resentment will build and discontentment will set in. As a result, some people exist in a continuously suppressed state, feeling constantly frustrated but not knowing why, while others, unable to suppress the frustration, reach bursting point with varying degrees of severity and use that energy to drive change in a forceful way.

## Rules

Life appears to be simpler when we are given a set of rules to follow that have been set by someone else. 'Tell me the rules, I will stick by them. Then I won't get into trouble.' Those rules could include, for example, the company's office hours and dress code. But it is important for rule setters to distinguish which rules are helpful to all who will be expected to abide by them and which are based on a hierarchical preference. There is a difference between a rule that serves the workplace because, for example, setting office hours means everyone party to a task is in the office at the same time, and setting a random rule that simply tells everyone to wear blue without explaining what purpose this serves.

If a rule doesn't serve a purpose that can be understood by everyone expected to comply with it, then conflicts arise because if the reason for getting everyone to wear blue is only that the person in authority prefers blue, resentment will set in. If there is no authentic forum to allow employees to express their resentment, some people will address the balance in other ways, such as cheating. But, if the reason for wearing blue is part of a carefully thought out strategy that will increase the success of the organization and therefore increase the likelihood of continued employment, then more people will want to participate willingly because they can find meaning and purpose in complying.

The point is that everyone should be able to see how a rule makes life better. If they can't see that, problems will arise. One form of industrial action is to 'Work to Rule' where employees do no more than the minimum required by the rules of their contract and then follow the rules excessively. This generally demonstrates how much a system relies on discretion and goodwill.

### Breaking the Rules

Unnecessary complexities arise when the very people who set the rules break those rules themselves, creating a double standard. Examples of this are prevalent in commerce, government and religion. People who have been bullied by a boss will know this only too well.

---

### Rational Rule Breaking

I have a system I call 'rational rule breaking' where I break a rule because it makes sense to do so – for example, I allow a team member to come in late so he/she can wait in for the plumber and I let the other team members know I am exercising discretion in allowing this. A key factor in this system is that the same discretion is extended to everyone, based on ongoing trust and building dialogue with the team. The alternative is that someone is afraid to ask to come in late because they fear punishment, and cheat instead by coming in late and pretending they were on a work appointment. The more staunch an organization is about keeping rules to the letter and not allowing discretion, the more cheating actually goes on – and the easiest way to create dishonest people is to mistrust them.

---

It's hard to take rules seriously when they are made by people who are not likely to obey the rules themselves and when they are imposed on people who also don't keep to them. This is really common and yet we rarely challenge it. For example, patent law was intended to inspire inventiveness but rich firms often buy up patents and suppress the products to stop competition. And often, when the rules do not achieve the desired effect, more rules are made. There has been a

long-term trend in the UK for each new government to legis-
late more aggressively than its predecessors and yet crime,
and more importantly fear of crime, is still with us.

Look at any workplace and you will see that people break
rules all the time, from the global banking crisis to someone
taking home a paperclip. But the addiction to controlling or
regulating groups is everywhere – especially in workplaces.

If there is no dialogue or collaboration, rules become about
compliance. Obeying rules becomes more important than
harmony between people. Once we stop discussing and start
imposing rules, there is an implicit message: 'You cannot be
trusted to make choices that are fair or to engage with others
and find something that works for everyone.' This contributes
to discontentment because trust is a really important need.

Sometimes the environment does not support change or
challenge to the rules without the use of force such as a strike.
It is important to your well-being to know what you can live
with and at what point you would walk away.

---

'Rules and norms also tend to be impressed into
the service of the Domination System, and to serve as a
form of crowd control rather than to enhance the
fullness of human potential.'

WALTER WINK (1935–2012)
KNOWN FOR HIS WORK ON POWER STRUCTURES

---

## Systemic Thinking

Systemic thinking helps us to understand interdependencies and how the individual elements are not isolated, but influence each other within a whole. Take the planet, for example – the air, the plants, the animals, the water and the earth all work together to sustain or destroy the whole. Before dealing with an issue, a systemic thinker views the 'problem' as part of an overall system and considers the consequences for the whole system before solving the local interruption – so before putting down pesticides as a solution to the local problem of bugs, the systemic thinker would consider the consequences to the bigger system and include that thinking in their decision.

In an organization, there are people and processes that need to work together collaboratively to flourish. You are part of that system. There may be limits to how much of the system you can influence or change on your own. However, this doesn't stop you from attending to yourself and really understanding where you fit into the bigger picture and whether it is for you, or not.

## ELIMINATING DISCONTENTMENT

*This book is about becoming better informed and then reflecting, reviewing and making balanced decisions and changes in a structured and joyful way. This is a self-responsible journey. You do this for yourself as part of being responsible for your own well-being.*

Y OU DO NOT NEED TO MAKE ANY EXTERNAL CHANGES until you have completed your learning. You will be taking a step back and observing your life at work and I will be guiding you through that process.

Very often a client will tell me how unhappy they are at work. Often by the time they make the choice to get support, the situation at work is in crisis. John was in this position. He had taken a new job but it was nothing like the job that had been advertised. He hated it but no one was listening, and he found himself at breaking point. To complicate matters, his line manager was having an affair with a director, a situation that left John feeling powerless to manoeuvre. His reaction to this put him into crisis. As we chatted through the problem, it became evident that he was now the one initiating hostile communication with his line manager.

Our early sessions were just a place for him to be heard and receive empathy. Once he was calmer, I guided him through a step-by-step process. First, he was able to understand his part in perpetuating the hostility. From that position he was able to transform the situation into one he could live with; then he made the decision to look for another job. This process took about twelve weeks. During that time I also encouraged him to examine conflict in his life – to identify the triggers and where else they appeared. Once out of crisis, and with a new perspective on his conflict management process, he was able to find another way of communicating with his manager, who responded by being supportive. He no longer wanted to leave and life settled down.

## Honing the Skill

It wasn't long before the beginnings of another crisis emerged with someone else at work, but we were able to catch it in time before it escalated. I asked John what it would be like to live life in a calm way for six months before effecting any

---

### A World Without Rules

If you are interested in a world with fewer rules, take a look at sociocracy – a method of designing harmonious organisations and workplaces based on the principle of consent. This means that all objections have been considered before a decision is reached. It was developed by Gerard Endenberg in order to help workplace relationships be peer relationships and not master, servant relationships.

---

change. He committed to doing so and it was quite hard for him. He recognized that his pattern of stirring things up arose because he was confusing calm with dull. He was using drama and crisis to energize himself. After six months he recognized how change did not need to come out of drama and could be a considered and enjoyable journey.

This journey took about a year. Most of it was 'unlearning'. When we have spent a long time doing things the same way, it takes time to undo them and find a new way.

## LOOKING INSIDE

◆

*Let's begin at the beginning with what is going on inside you. In the following exercise, you are going to discover how to open up an inner space for reflection. You'll start with breathing to relax and then you will examine what you tell yourself.*

THIS EXERCISE WILL REQUIRE you to have about twenty minutes of uninterrupted time. If that seems difficult, I'd like you to dig deep inside and challenge yourself with some questions:

- How sustainable is a life without adequate breaks?
- Are you depriving yourself of time for yourself?
- What would stepping off the treadmill feel like?
- If a dear friend needed twenty minutes of your time, would you squeeze it in?

- Now go deeper and ask yourself: 'What is it I am avoiding by keeping so busy?'
- If you are still convinced that you are so busy you cannot take twenty minutes of uninterrupted time to invest in yourself, could that be reason enough to make a change and take that time?

**Twenty Minutes**

Before you start, read through the whole exercise and plan how you will do it.

It will help if you can plan to be in a safe, comfortable space where you won't be disturbed or distracted. You can prepare for this time by making sure that any unfinished tasks will not intrude in your thoughts. This exercise requires you to become aware of sensations.

Allow ten minutes for the first part of the exercise – a breathing exercise, which is a common meditative technique in mindfulness practice. I will refer to this exercise several times throughout the book.

Sit comfortably on an upright chair with the soles of your feet flat on the floor, your spine straight and your head slightly bowed. Close your eyes and begin to consider how you breathe. Work towards evenness in the inhalation and exhalation and slow your breathing down by taking slightly longer over each breath, maintaining a rhythm that is entirely comfortable. Breathe down deep into the diaphragm. Focus on inhaling and exhaling and sense how your breathing affects other parts of your body. Notice your ribs moving in and out. Check for any tightness or heaviness in the shoulders, heart or stomach areas. Place your hands on any area of your body that is comforting and allow yourself to 'be' for the remainder of the ten minutes, and then just come round so that you are comfortable and aware but not alert. Do this part before reading on.

Now read through the next part of the exercise so that you are clear about what you are going to do and how to time it; and allow the next ten minutes as follows.

You are going to explore how you came to be who you are. Go back to your early years at school and reflect on the foundations of your school career. These are some questions you might consider:

- Who told you about going to school and how were you prepared for it?
- How did you experience your first years at school? Was it a happy time? Was it scary?
- What did you like about school?
- What did you dislike about school?
- Was interacting with other children easy or difficult?
- How did the adults behave towards you?
- What did they teach you about school as a community?
- Was that congruent with your experience?
- Did the adults practise what they preached?

Take some time to consider your answers. Your responses inform the start of how you shaped your personality to cope with the world. Now consider how this all feels. Answering the questions was a thinking process; now we're going into a feeling process. What do you feel when you immerse yourself in those answers? Here are some feeling words to help you:

*Sadness • Disappointment • Frustration • Anxiety • Guilt Shame • Resentment • Discontent • Happiness • Calm • Trust Delight • Joy • Satisfaction • Contentment.*

If you come up with your own words, try to ensure you are using words that describe a feeling – 'I feel…'.

Notice what is happening as you allow yourself to feel the feelings. Place your hands wherever gives you comfort, connect with your breathing again and just allow it to be whatever it is before coming back to an awake state. As you come out of the exercise, reflect on how easy it was to do and assess how easy or difficult it is going to be for you to read this book and change the things in your work life that are not working for you. You might want to think about a timescale for change or a plan for incremental steps towards change.

**Your Story**

Think about an event or an incident that happened when you were a child where the outcome, in the hands of adults, left you unhappy. It might have happened to you or someone you know. Here's an example from my childhood. I remember

being in class at seven years old and given coloured squares of paper. We were asked to stick the coloured squares of paper point to point on a larger sheet of paper. I was quite pleased with what I had created. I liked the pattern and the colours. However, when the teacher came round she told me my work was untidy – I hadn't noticed, but the points of some squares were overlapping. She started shouting and then slapped me and physically shook me in my seat. This was over forty years ago and nowadays, of course, such a physical discipline wouldn't be allowed. But, regardless of era, I was still a child of seven who didn't understand what was happening. I couldn't have known then that I was simply being used as a stooge for her to release some frustration in her life. I was feeling shock and humiliation. Teachers at my school often used humiliation to modify behaviour. And when this was repeated over and again, I learned to expect it as part of life.

Once you have remembered a story, stick with it. It is your narrative, a vehicle for expressing your feelings and needs. Take time to consider the aspects of what happened and how the events affected everyone involved. Then consider the other people involved and ask yourself whether they would have the same perspective or attach the same importance.

I can guess that the real source of unhappiness in your narrative was the absence of fairness. Fairness and justice are important needs. We hold those needs individually for ourselves and also collectively for communities we participate in.

Now think about another incident or event at work where you were left feeling unhappy with the conclusion or result. It's a safe bet that here, too, you will find unfairness at the root of unhappiness. We can tell ourselves that it's an unjust world and we shouldn't expect fairness; but it eats away at us.

## Coping with Constructs of Society

When everything is going well at work, we tend not to dwell on the reasons because we take it for granted; but when things are not going well at work and we feel down about it, we search for coping strategies to get us through.

We did a lot of learning about how to cope when we were at school. We worked out the personalities of the teachers and we adjusted and modified our behaviour as best we could to avoid getting into trouble – and to see what we could get away with. We developed a coping strategy for each situation. When work is dissatisfying, we repeat our coping strategy until we can't take any more.

The school system we use in the West was invented to create a constant stream of compliant factory workers in response to the Industrial Revolution. The system was sold to industrialists on the basis that children could be made to be more compliant and productive by teaching them to be obe-dient. Large-scale education programmes were designed to churn out adults who would fit into a system. And just like it is virtually impossible to stick to all the rules all the time, it is

also virtually impossible to remain compliant and obedient all the time; but when your livelihood is at stake, it can be very difficult to challenge what is in front of you. The resulting frustration leaks out of us in other aspects of our life where we consider there is less at stake — such as shouting at the family because you can't shout at the boss; driving the car in a rage because you can't show rage in the workplace; drinking more alcohol than is good for you, as an anaesthetic; and complaining about work to anyone outside work who will listen. When work begins to affect other areas of your life, it's important to reflect on why we allow this to happen. Mindfulness helps us to do this and to find a proper perspective.

## THE SYSTEMS OF SOCIETY

*When people come together to meet a common aim, we usually create a system to help us organize. Sometimes the systems are not really fit for purpose and it takes a strong leader to effect change.*

I N THIS BOOK, I HAVE REFERRED TO OUR CHILDHOODS and to school. Society creates systems to organize the people within it — for example, there are educational systems, cultural systems and economic systems. Businesses operate within the economic system. Within a business there are systems to manage the business and largely those systems are out of step with the social issues, which are as present at work as

they are outside it. For example, in some jobs it is entirely possible for the work to be structured around a person's life, but the employer might dictate that the person's life is structured around the work because the system cannot adapt. For a system to be useful, it needs to sustain all its participants. If it can't, then the system is less useful than it could be.

Ask yourself whether the systems you are engaged in are really fit for purpose and how chained you are to them. Any system simply compromises a group of people who promote a way of doing things and it's important to see how, once it becomes difficult to change a system, it is probably already unfit for purpose.

---

## Reflections

I called this chapter 'Wake Up and Smell the Coffee' because the phrase means to pay attention and do something about a situation. You bought this book because you want to improve your work situation, probably for a variety of reasons. In order to do that, you will need to pay attention and become mindful about what your situation really is. While you are probably able to describe with ease what is not working for you, my hope in this chapter is to help you recognize some of the systemic problems that contribute towards so much unhappiness at work.

# CHAPTER TWO

# FREEDOM &
# SUSTAINABILITY

*Finding a balance between freedom
to do as we please and earning an income to
sustain ourselves can become a tightrope. Without
mindful thinking, it's all too easy to find yourself
caught in a trap, believing money is the obstacle
and unable to escape. In this chapter, we examine
the choices we made, the consequences of those
choices, and how all the messages for change are
right in front of us if we are awake to what is
around us. Mindfulness helps us explore the
beliefs that led us to make those choices.*

# THE TRAP

◆

*One of the most common traps we fall into is feeling stuck and one of the most common ways we make ourselves stuck is by struggling to keep within our comfort zone instead of actively moving to the edges in a structured and informed way.*

A VERY DEAR FRIEND AND I used to meet regularly to visit an art exhibition as a source of creative inspiration. In 2005 we visited the Serpentine Gallery in London and took our chances on whatever was on show, which turned out to be an exhibition by Andreas Slominski. I'd never heard of him before then, but that particular exhibition has stuck with me ever since. Slominski has gained a reputation as an artistic trickster and is best known for the series of traps he has designed and made since the 1980s. The traps are all constructed to catch prey, from insects to monkeys. They are all different in form, structure and complexity. The traps are displayed as installations and the viewer is invited to scrutinize them from all angles in order to figure out how they would work. In that process the viewer is also trapped – no longer just a viewer, he or she has been drawn into engagement with the work, studying the intricacies of the design while blindly ignoring the fact that he or she is participating in the study of a killing machine. It's only after we have embroiled ourselves in something that we see how caught up we have become.

## What Do You Do for a Living?

For many people, work is a trap that crept up on them and the majority would not continue doing the same work if they could access the money to live on without working for it. When we are young, the adults around us are intent on us securing our future – either through education or getting a good job – and once we buy into their fear of our destitution, it's easy to get caught up in a system that fights off poverty but doesn't invite abundance. It is very difficult to get out of that thinking, especially when you have built an entire lifestyle around your work and define yourself by your job. During my transition from a 'businesswoman' working to avoid destitution to someone who embraces living, I became acutely aware of a club I had unconsciously joined; I noticed that any social introduction was immediately followed by: 'What do you do for a living?' I was trapped in thinking that was an innocent question. Once I began to consider my life at work and started to explore other ways of being, I realized it was a highly loaded question. It's a means of judging people by what they do for a living and deciding whether they are part of my club.

---

'It is our choices ... that show what we
truly are, far more than our abilities.'

J.K. ROWLING
AUTHOR

---

## Leaving the Club

Part of my waking up happened when I gradually got to know the father of my son's friend. From time to time our paths would cross, as they do when you ferry your small children to parties and school events. Of course, I asked him the question: 'What do you do for a living?' I don't remember his answer but I remember mentally dismissing him because he wasn't 'one of us'. He wasn't 'in business'. But we would come across each other from time to time and I would listen benignly to things that were incomprehensible to me about his work, which was in the 'not-for-profit' sector. It turned out he was one of my life's messengers. He was inviting me to explore a way of being in the world that wasn't money driven; but I couldn't hear it. One day he invited me to a workshop on Nonviolent Communication (NVC) and I arrogantly said yes as a favour to help him out by buying a ticket. On the day, I thought about cancelling – after all, I had paid for my ticket so no harm done – but I asked myself what I could lose from attending and the answer was 'Nothing'. That event was the turning point in my decision-making process about how to change what I was doing. Learning for the first time about NVC, I understood what drove me to challenge so much of what I experienced in the world and how the way I was challenging it was not helping.

*...I understood what drove me to challenge so much of what I experienced in the world...*

## RECOGNIZING YOUR MESSENGERS

◆

*It's easy to be stuck in a groove and unable to step back. Much of the time we are so caught up in our day-to-day struggles that we cannot hear what others are telling us or receive their messages.*

IN THIS EXERCISE you are going to practise recognizing your messengers. Start with the breathing exercise from Chapter One. By doing this regularly, you're creating a space for transitioning from the mindless day-to-day to a time of mindfulness.

Now think about all the people close to you. What have they been saying to you that you have ignored, dismissed, got angry about, or reacted badly to? Take time to be thorough. I will demonstrate using an example from my own life.

*A good example for me was how much my children complained about me being on my mobile phone. I rationalized this as conducting business, which paid for our family trips and holidays.*

Choose one of those people. Imagine this person is a helpful messenger, dressed appropriately. Surround them with light and beauty and imagine that they have only one intention – to support you to find your higher self and to be abundant.

*In my example I took my son and remembered a photo of him at the age of two, when he looked like a cherub.*

Now translate their message into words that support you. Look beyond their criticism and hear a positive message in their words that would support you in becoming happier.

*For me, the original message 'Why do you always have to answer
your phone?' translated into 'Mum, I'm sure you would be
happier if you could find a way to give yourself space and
time to enjoy family life'.*

It's a difficult exercise because we expose the ways in which
we haven't been kind to ourselves when we translate the message. Work through as many people and messages as you can.
It can be a revelation to discover all the messengers of goodwill in your life. They just can't express it clearly because our
social conditioning developed our use of language for competing, not collaborating. It takes all parties to a conversation
to collaborate and understand what is being communicated
and to try and uncover the message beneath the message.

As you become proficient at this exercise, you will begin to
learn about the many opportunities to do things differently
that are on your doorstep – or even closer to home.

## WORK / LIFE BALANCE

Achieving a work/life balance does not mean equal time for
both. It is a fluid proposition that changes and fluctuates
according to the demands being made on you and how you
meet them. You achieve balance when you have the integrated
self-responsibility to meet your obligations while also having
the confidence to set boundaries that keep your life rewarding.

## ESCAPING THE TRAP

◆

*We've all thought about what we would do if we won the lottery, then write these thoughts off as escapism — but actually those thoughts illustrate our struggle to find an easy way out of the trap.*

RECENTLY, I BUMPED INTO the eighteen-year-old son of a friend of mine. I chatted with him for a while and could tell something was wrong; and when I commented that he seemed upset, his eyes filled with tears. He had just heard that he had failed his exams and his parents were furious with him. He told me he wasn't that worried because he had already considered the alternatives and planned to join a group of artists and experiment with his creative talents, but his parents were in outrage and insisting he get a job in a local factory.

I told him to follow his heart and also to find a way to have compassion for his parents, and to help them to be calm about the situation. I said that growing up was about finding ways to be in the world that do not alienate others, while still being true to oneself, and about being self-responsible. I didn't want him to begin the journey into a trap of living up to other people's expectations and buying into the fear of destitution, never having explored his own inner passion for the world.

There's a good probability that you are reading this book because you are already some way down the track. If that's the case, there is some unlearning to do.

## What Would You Do?

What would you do if you could access enough money to live on without working and it was guaranteed for as long as you wanted it? Take a little time to reflect on this. If your answer contains even the smallest difference between what you do now and what you *would* do, ask yourself what's in the way of doing it now. If the answer has anything to do with money, then you are caught in a trap. The point of recognizing this is that often when people are caught in a trap, they panic and react, making decisions that make the trap more painful.

When I asked myself what I would do if the money I needed to live on was 'on tap', I noticed that I would continue to run my charity and continue to see clients, and I would free up more time to do this because I would not need to spend so much time earning money. I would simply give more time to people on lower incomes who would like my help and I would put more time into proving the model of community participation that I am keen to develop. When I asked myself 'Why not just do it now?', my answer was that I had made a considered choice to maintain a lifestyle. I used to think it was money, until I realized I was in a trap. The process of making informed choices took me through a complete career change and into deeper questions about how much money was enough.

*...I had made a considered choice
to maintain a lifestyle.*

## MONEY, MONEY, MONEY

We can't ignore money because it plays such a big role in our lives. We spend a lot of time thinking about it; how to acquire it, how to save it and how to spend it. While it is never far from our thoughts, we rarely spend time considering our relationship with it and how different it is for some people than others. And many of us don't really know what it is.

## Relating to Money

I was interested to explore what we teach children about money and research revealed that children are taught a lot about spending, saving, budgeting and earning in a way that is relevant to their age. That is the practical stuff. I didn't see much being taught about where money comes from. It's important to understand that banks create money by lending it. Every time someone borrows, more money is created, and more money is lent out than banks hold in reserve. Banks prefer to lend against collateral so that if the loan goes wrong they can swap their created money for your very real house. Of course it didn't start out like that. Originally the money represented an amount of gold and was an iou from the bank that held the gold. But money became such a powerful force that we lost sight of the original purpose and became obsessed with the notes, so naturally they took on their own meaning.

When you really examine this, it means that money is based on a belief system that only works because everyone joins in and joining in is a choice. You might feel your choices are limited because you fear that not joining in will put you in a worse position; but until you have tried reducing your reliance on a system that causes a lot of suffering and misery, you cannot say for sure what the outcomes will be. For example, some people up and leave the mainstream system and flourish because they have the combination of self-responsibility and confidence to create a life that meets their needs. Others make changes when they reach a point of feeling they have nothing to lose, which can lead to success or the need to rethink; and yet others make their way perfectly well and lead a healthy, balanced life within the current systems. No one knows better what is right for you than you – but the best way to work out what to do is through an informed choice.

## Alternative Sustainability

Once you are trapped into thinking that money is the answer to your problems, you have missed the point of finding sustainability. Money is a part of a strategy for meeting needs.

---

'Freedom … is more than just a seven letter word.'

VERONICA CHAPMAN
ACTIVIST

---

The need might be food, shelter, adventure or relaxation, for example; but money is simply one way of accessing those things. For example, in bartering systems no money is needed and people access what they need by trading time, skills or goods. Gifting is another system being explored by some groups, where a community discusses what is needed for sustaining itself and everyone gives freely with no expectation of receiving. These systems require trust and compassion, not competition and rivalry. It comes out of a completely different way of viewing the world.

Of course, money exists, and I am not suggesting that you should do anything different if you are content or have weighed up the risks and decided to stay put. If, however, you want to consider change, I am inviting you to think beyond what is normal to you and embrace the suggestion that other ways of being on the planet exist and are successful.

Discontentment grew when we were encouraged to build lifestyles based on the acquisition of money and were then persuaded to want bigger and better lifestyles. So we were given credit to have the lifestyle in advance of acquiring the wealth to pay for it. If you are caught in that trap, you are probably unhappy or stressed or both. Probably you dream of breaking free and imagine a time when you won't be in this position – so you keep working hard at it to free yourself, when in actual fact you are painting yourself ever further into a corner; release will require some radical new thinking.

Once you can understand how you have painted yourself into a corner, the first realization I would like you to come to terms with is that you will not work your way out of it in one step. You will need a plan. And the first part of that plan is identifying what it is you want. This is all about change. You are reading this book because you want to feel better about your work, and just wanting to feel better requires change. So you need to think about the things that are in your control to change and the things that are out of your control to change.

Some people have fewer options for getting access to money than others. The question remains as to whether you want to invest your energies in chasing money to stay afloat or whether there are other ways to live that involve less reliance on money. I met a couple who impressed me deeply. Having been in prison, the husband's job choices were very limited, and because he was an ex-prisoner, he was not treated with respect when he did find work, so he seemed destined to live on welfare benefits. This caused a strain on the marriage and they almost broke up. They decided to do volunteering as a couple. They volunteered to cook all the food in a community kitchen five days a week. They have accepted a life with virtually no money with complete joy because, as volunteers, they feel they are giving freely and are equals in the organization. They now have a standing in the community and have gained respect and love, which has given them greater confidence in themselves. They would not swap their life for anything.

## THE WAY IT IS

◆

*You were born into your society and the educational, cultural and economic systems already in place. You were trained to follow those systems. While the system works for you everything is great. If you bump up against the edges of the system, life becomes unpleasant.*

REMAINING WITHIN ANY SYSTEM IS A CHOICE. When you were a child, you relied on adults to make those choices for you. As an adult, it is vital that you understand that you choose your life and that, while options for some are more limited, you still choose your attitude to it all. Your decision to be part of a system (or not) is based on what you perceive you may lose or gain and what you believe to be at stake. Reasons for participating in a system may include:

- Fear of finding yourself worse off.
- The perceived benefits outweighing the losses.
- You don't know any other way.
- You don't trust anyone can help you with another way.
- You like the way it is and can live with any disadvantages.
- You want to continue with this group.
- You believe that continuing will pay off in the future.
- You believe you can change the system from the inside.
- You don't want to disappoint some people you know.
- You are ashamed of telling people you are unhappy.
- You can't imagine being happy.

This list isn't exhaustive. If you are unhappy with your work situation for any reason, take a moment and ask yourself what stops you changing it right now. You might want to revisit the section on resistance (see pages 20–1). You have to be honest with yourself here and get past the superficial reasons, which are generally grounded in assumptions and fears.

## Everything is a Choice

The hardest reality to face is that everything is a choice. However you are today, you chose it. I agree that circumstances will arise that seem to limit your options – being made redundant may not feel like a choice. The choice I am talking about is what you do in response to whatever obstacle comes in your way. There's a popular proverb that says 'when life gives you lemons, make lemonade'. That is an attitude and a skill. Learning the skills helps to develop the attitude. It means allowing yourself to fully mourn your losses but not allowing the feelings to disempower you from taking charge of your life. If you struggle with this reality, it's because you haven't yet learned to take full responsibility for the consequences and outcomes of your life. In a society where compliance and obedience to the rules are held up as the right way to live, it can be difficult to take responsibility because the changes you might want to make may require more from you emotionally and physically than you can find in yourself. This is where learning the skills of mindfulness will help to resource you.

When I get the opportunity to work with teachers, nurses or other caring professionals, I hear that there are many things they would do differently if they wrote 'the rule book', but they care about their clients, students or patients and choose to continue doing the work because, for them, that contribution is important. Very often they feel stressed and undervalued because they feel forced to continue doing things they disagree with. However, the point I am making is that the first step in finding contentment at work is realizing the choices you make and how you adapt to an imperfect job. If you don't truly understand that when you do things you disagree with you are choosing to compromise your own values for some other type of gain, you are writing yourself a prescription for ongoing misery at work.

**Reaction Versus Response**

Every action we take is a choice and everything we don't do is also a choice. Following the rules is a choice. We might choose it because our fear of being punished is greater than we can cope with, but nonetheless it is a choice. How do you make those choices? What level of awareness are you operating at? Are you simply reacting or are you truly responding? This is where mindfulness comes in. To be mindful, you develop awareness of the present moment-by-moment choices you are making that contribute to how your life is, and this may enable you to confront your learned helplessness.

## Learned Helplessness

One of the ways people are encouraged to follow the rules is on the promise that if they follow the rules they cannot be blamed if it goes wrong. That seems like an attractive proposition, but it creates learned helplessness. When I went to my daughter's graduation at Cambridge University, the whole family attended. It was an important day for us. My eighty-three-year-old mother was in a wheelchair. When we arrived, the security man told us that only one person could go with my mother to the wheelchair section. I attempted to have a conversation with the man about how important it was for us to do this as a family, since some members had come from overseas. The man could not hear me. He simply repeated the words 'Health and Safety' at me over and over again, as if I would then magically let go of attempting to find some humanity in the situation. I wanted him to use discretion – but the system he was working under did not allow that, and he chose to uphold that system. He might not even have been aware that he had a choice – but nonetheless it *was* a choice and he couldn't articulate it.

This is a good example of learned helplessness. More aware responses could have been: 'I can see this is difficult for your family but I am worried about losing my job so I'm choosing not to go against my remit' or 'What you are asking is past my remit and I don't know what to do' or 'I haven't been given authority to deal with this, let me find someone who has'.

There have been many experiments on learned helpless-ness where an animal is repeatedly hurt by something it cannot control. After a while the animal stops trying to avoid the pain and resigns itself to the situation. Thereafter, when opportunities are presented for escape the animal continues to remain in position and puts up with the pain. Experiments have also been conducted with humans, and one significant difference emerged: people can learn to be helpless just from watching other people be powerless.

Learned helplessness is what results from being instructed to mindlessly follow a system even when it is detrimental to its users; they cannot see any way to influence change and so they don't try. From a work perspective, the system could be a profession, an institution or a company. Systems are usually developed to serve a specific purpose and to make things easier for people. Over time, though, as the upholders of a system increasingly prioritize upholding it, such as enforcing a set lunchtime when a flexible lunchtime would work better for the team, the original purpose – which is for a team to feel happy and empowered to give their best – becomes decreasingly important until the system becomes 'the way things are done' unless there is a significant challenge.

Undoing learned helplessness is a process in mindfulness. It's not about jumping up, downing tools and rising up against rules; it's about recognizing the choices we've made in rela-tion to our circumstances and choosing what to change.

### Understanding Your Needs

Take some time to unwind using the breathing exercise in Chapter One (see pages 33–4).

Look at the list of needs you might want to fulfil through work. Pick out the top three or four that are most important to you. Now look at each need individually and work out whether that need is met or unmet in your life. Ask yourself the following questions and reflect on your answers:

- How does this need get met in my life?
- How do I contribute to this need being unmet in my life?
- What might it cost me to get this need met?
- Is there another way to get this need met that doesn't cost me anything?
- How might the people around me feel about the way I am meeting my needs?
- What needs of theirs might be met or unmet by my strategies?
- If I choose to let this need go unmet, how do I live joyfully with that choice?

You might consider journaling your answers so you can check back at a later date and see if you're succeeding in meeting your needs, or if indeed those needs are changing.

## Undoing Learned Helplessness

Undoing learned helplessness has three stages:

**1.** *Understand what it is you want.*

**2.** *Learn the skills to help you get what you want.*

**3.** *Remove the obstacles.*

Let's break that down...

*Understand What it is You Want*

Simply saying 'I want to get a new job' will not suffice. You might end up with a new job that is worse than the previous one. You need to take time to understand what the real problem is with your current work. And if you believe that someone else is to blame for the problem, you can be pretty sure you have a lot of work to do. Explore what needs of yours are being met or unmet by the current situation. We work for lots of different reasons. Here's a suggestion for some needs that might be fulfilled by working:

- Acknowledgement
- Appreciation
- Autonomy
- Challenge
- Collaboration
- Communication
- Competence
- Contact
- Contribution
- Cooperation
- Creativity
- Freedom
- Inclusion
- Independence
- Learning
- Meaning
- Participation
- Power
- Purpose
- Recognition
- Security
- Structure
- Sustenance

Now let's assume that your most important need is autonomy. You want to be your own person and earn your own money and make your own choices. To achieve this you set out to find a job and you take a full-time position in an organization where the rules are the rules and the process is the process and you have very little autonomy. You are spending most of your time not meeting your most important need in order to try to meet it. You know this, but you tell yourself that it's only work and you can shove that aside because it gets you what you want in your personal life. However, you will need to consider just how sustainable that position is.

Let's continue with the theme of autonomy. You now realize that autonomy is important – but how *much* autonomy is important to you? Is there a trust issue underlying this? At what point is meeting your need for autonomy detrimental to meeting one of your other needs? For example, would meeting your need for autonomy affect your need for inclusion? Would others feel less inclined to include you if you didn't take any notice of them in your decision-making? Maybe, when you consider this, the level of pain you feel when your need for autonomy goes unmet is not as great because inclusion is also important. You could choose to let go of some of your strategies for meeting your need for autonomy in order to be included. This is choosing. Until you understand yourself and can make choices that fit with who you really are, you won't know what it is you really want.

*Learn the Skills to Help You Get What You Want*

By doing the exercises in this book, you will learn some of the cognitive and emotional skills needed to become mindful, to take self-responsibility, and to make informed choices. Your first task is to recognize and overcome your own negative patterns and cycles – otherwise they will remain with you even if you achieve your dream of, for example, moving to the country and raising chickens, and as soon as you hit an obstacle you will revert to your familiar coping mechanisms. Alternatively, you might benefit from learning a practical skill – you might, for example, decide to remain in your job for the moment and meet your need for self-expression by learning about how to write a novel; in this way you will find contentment in the present while working towards the future.

---

## REFLECTIONS

In this chapter, I set out to cut through the beliefs and limitations that often hold us back. I wanted you to discover that money is not a need. It is a strategy for meeting needs and one that most of mainstream society participates in. I also wanted you to learn that participation is a choice and to see how we juggle different needs and priorities. If we are not mindful in this process, we can cause ourselves unnecessary unhappiness.

CHAPTER THREE

# THE HONEST AUDIT

*What is actually happening in your work and
your workplace? How are you inclined to interpret
and perceive what goes on? This chapter is about how
the lens through which you look at life affects what
you see and hear. We will look at whether what you see
and hear is really accurate by examining the difference
between message sent and message received, in order to
gain a better understanding of what was meant, what
actually occurred, and how it left everyone feeling.
We'll explore the culture of a workplace and become
mindful about your place in that culture.*

## THE POSITIVE & THE NEGATIVE

◆

*Some of us lean towards a negative or pessimistic perception of what is going on around us, while others lean towards a positive or optimistic perception. How you perceive your role and your workplace depends on how your experiences have affected you.*

SOME TIME AGO I was doing a presentation about my work at a meeting of schools liaison officers from the police force. Their role was to visit high schools and engage with the pupils and staff by advising on police work, supporting the school to fight crime and building community relations. I asked this group what they most liked about the job and they all said the best bit was working nine to five and not having to do shifts. I could see how that might be very attractive to a person who has chosen a job that mostly involves shift work.

On another occasion I was doing a consultation with a group of disgruntled youth workers. They were very angry about the way they were being treated by the management – but when I asked if there was anything they liked about the job, they all said that the internal politics and management heartache became less important when a wayward young person found another path as a result of their intervention.

I also did some training with a group of senior executives in the design team of a large corporate company. Their motivations were very different. Some were ambitious and wanted

## YOUR MAGNIFYING GLASS

Grab a magnifying glass or imagine you are holding one. Sit down and place the magnifying glass over a nearby object. This could be a pen or a mobile phone or a credit card. Notice any flaws or imperfections on the object that might be less visible without the magnifying glass. Now, leaving the object where it is, stand up and look at the object again through the magnifying glass, from a greater distance, and see how the view of it differs. Now elevate yourself even higher (if you can do so safely) by standing on a chair, and look again through the magnifying glass. The object is still there but it is small in the context of the bigger view you now have.

Life is the same. You choose where you put your magnifying glass. You choose what bothers you. You choose what to address, what to ignore and what to resolve. Of course, the three-dimensional world influences you and impacts you — but you are not determined by it. You have the choice and the personal power to determine your own reality. Our stories help us make sense of the events and incidents that affect us but the stories are vehicles that contain the essence of how we view the world and the people in it. How we tell ourselves that story can determine our misery or our happiness.

to climb the career ladder; others were comfortable with the job security of a large organization; and yet others were motivated by seeing their creative ideas transformed into high street recognition.

---

'We must look at the lens through which we see
the world, as well as the world we see, and that the lens
itself shapes how we interpret the world.'

STEPHEN R. COVEY
AUTHOR OF 'THE 7 HABITS OF HIGHLY EFFECTIVE PEOPLE'

---

## Accentuating the Positive

We all have different reasons for doing what we do, and no matter how bad it is, there are always some positives. Take a couple of minutes to reflect on your work and workplace. Start with what you like about it. Jot down any positives about your job, the people you work with, the environment and the end results. Focus on those positive outcomes. Spend some time allowing yourself to feel the feelings of having those positives. If that is difficult to do, it's probably because you are paying a high price for those things. We will address that later – there will be a reckoning; but for now, set it aside. Just imagine those positives, whether they are for self-centred reasons, like the schools liaison officers or the corporate executives, or for reasons of contribution, like the youth workers. In all cases, if you draw any benefits from doing what you do, those are self-centred reasons – which, in this context, means you are trying to take care of yourself, and this is a good thing.

Hopefully there is more than one positive in your work life and, if so, start to prioritize those positives. Then identify what need is being met by each positive you've identified. Your list might look similar to this:

- THE JOB IS NEAR HOME (NO COMMUTING) = needs met
  *ease and simplicity*
- THE JOB STRETCHES ME = needs met
  *challenge and competence*
- THE JOB PAYS WELL = needs met
  *sustainability and security*

Now concentrate on the needs that are being met. How does it feel to have those needs met? Do you feel pleasure, pride, joy or something else? Take some time to enjoy these feelings. Allow them to wash over you. Of course, there are probably some negatives to your current position and we will work with those; but it is important to bring the good stuff into consciousness as often as possible in order to remember that life is never all bad. It might seem that the bad outweighs the good but it shouldn't diminish it and you can choose what you focus on. Take some time to remember what is working for

*Spend some time allowing yourself to feel the feelings of having those positives.*

you by connecting with the needs that are met in your life and celebrate the part of you that wants to flourish and is capable of finding ways to meet your needs. Remember that you choose what you tell yourself and it is important to find a balance in those messages.

## Extracting the Negative

Now let's address the negative side of your work situation. Take a couple of minutes to reflect on your work and workplace. Work on what you don't like about it. Jot down any negatives about your job, the people you work with, the environment and the end results. As in the previous exercise on the positive aspects, think about what needs are *not* being met and jot down a similar list, which might look like this:

- NOT ENOUGH BREAKS = needs not met
  *rest, calm and balance*
- COLLEAGUES ARE IN CONFLICT = needs not met
  *harmony and cooperation*
- TOO MUCH PAPERWORK = needs not met
  *effectiveness and simplicity*

---

'People do not seem to realize that their opinion of the
world is also a confession of character.'

RALPH WALDO EMERSON (1803–1882)
LEADER OF THE TRANSCENDENTALIST MOVEMENT

---

## WHAT ARE YOU REALLY REACTING TO?

*Sometimes we think we are dealing with the problem in front of us, when in actual fact we are trying to resolve an issue that persists in our life. This means our reactions may seem disproportionate to the person in front of us, which then escalates the issue.*

CHLOE HAD BEEN MISERABLE AT WORK. She came to see me in a state. She is a high achiever, always exceeding her performance targets. Her pattern is always the same. She takes a new job, full of enthusiasm and creativity. The new job always starts well. She gets on well with her colleagues, meets her targets and the senior management is impressed.

Then she starts to do two things. First, she begins to contribute ideas on how things could be better and second, because she does her job so well and believes she has earned the right to speak out against injustices she sees, she protests against unfairness. For example, when a manager moved the weekly team meeting to the end of the day, she pointed out that staff with childcare responsibilities would be put under unnecessary pressure. At this point, she is seen as a threat – usually by a manager who is resistant to her feedback – and a power struggle begins. From Chloe's point of view, her need for respect is not being met so she kicks harder. When this fails to gain respect and results in even more hostility, she gets another job – and repeats the cycle elsewhere.

'Insanity is doing the same thing over
and over again and expecting different results.'

ALBERT EINSTEIN (1879–1955)
NOBEL PRIZE WINNER

Chloe gave me her account of her life at work and explained how she had started yet another new job. She had reached the point where she recognized that the situation was repeating itself and she was the common denominator. She realized she could influence the outcome by changing her behaviour.

The really important part of this story is that every time the cycle repeated itself, the intensity was greater and her sense that the situation was taking over her life became over-whelming. She hadn't understood that she was not responding to the single incident in front of her in the present, but to the fifty times it had happened before and she had been unable to get a positive result. Her habitual 'fight or flight' mechanism kicked in because she saw the problem as external and, until now, had been unable to see how she kept repeating an old pattern over and over again. Same drama, different actors...

**Your Story**

Now let's find out whether you have a pattern or an unre-solved issue that crops up in your life from time to time. Find a friend whose values and opinions you respect and who is willing to spend some time working with you on the positives and negatives of your situation. Let's assume that your friend is called Sam. Ask Sam to follow a set of simple instructions and to say or do nothing but what is asked and not go off on tangents. Read through the exercise first; then allow about twenty minutes to work through it.

Ask Sam to do nothing but listen and to maintain some eye contact with you but not to interrupt or ask any questions until you have finished speaking.

Tell Sam about all the things you feel unhappy about in your work life. Avoid thinking too much about it – just allow the story to spill out however it comes.

When you have finished, ask Sam to reflect back to you what you said. Listen carefully to Sam; this is the message that he has received or 'heard'. It will probably be a little different to what you intended and it may require you to explain further.

Now, between you, work on the difference between what you said (the message sent) and what Sam reflected back (the message received). Sam may need to ask some questions to get to a mutual understanding, for example:

- *How does that feel?*
- *Can you explain…?*
- *What was going on for you at the time?*
- *How does this affect you?*
- *Who else was involved?*
- *What would you have preferred?*

Questions framed in this way help because they allow both of you to go beyond the story and identify the underlying issues.

Continue until you feel there is a mutual understanding of your situation. This is not as easy as it sounds. Sam must remain focused on you and your story. You are using a dialogue to establish what the real issues are for you. This is not a forum for Sam to interrogate you or make a judgement.

Once you have reached a mutual understanding of your situation, ask Sam to comment on the situation but not to give you any advice – this is really important. Helpful comments might be 'This must be a very difficult situation' or 'There are many people involved so I wonder if you are

---

### WHY DID YOU DO THAT?

Asking someone 'why' usually causes that person to feel defensive and leads to a justification or excuse, which is not the same as an explanation. Such questions do not help in the process of reaching mutual understanding of a situation. Examples of questions that might be interpreted as inflammatory include:

- *Why did you do that?*
- *What was the point of that?*
- *What do you think of what you did?*
- *What do you think of what they said?*

---

finding it complex?' or 'I guess this is frustrating for you?'. Unhelpful comments are 'The same thing happened to me' or 'Here's why this has gone wrong' or 'In your shoes I would…'.

*You could be feeling differently about the problem, about yourself or about others involved.*

Once you have completed the listening exercise, reached a mutual understanding of your situation and Sam has given you feedback, check yourself and see what has shifted. You could be feeling differently about the problem, about yourself or about others involved. Tell Sam about anything that has changed from when you started out the exercise, say thank you, and end the exercise with some acknowledgement of gratitude or love for Sam's friendship.

## Understanding Your Reality

During the above exercise, something in you will have shifted, however small. Often undertaking this exercise can shift a person's whole perception. The point of doing it is to see how, in that time of reflecting, you did not change anything external. The situation is still the same but your position on it changed and that made something different. When you understand this fully, you begin to see how your life is self-determining. Once you grasp that, you become in charge of your own destiny.

## SEARCHING FOR BALANCE

Balance is an interesting proposition. We talk about the work/life balance as if it is the golden prize. Not having it is another reason to feel guilty and generate lots of self-blame for not being masters of all the demands that are made on us. Much of the stress and anxiety we feel comes from feeling inadequate. It comes from believing we have to be better at life than we are. Most of what upsets us is the sense that we should be able to balance everything. I often pack my day with numerous activities I want to participate in, and also tasks I hate but I want to do to support order in my life. All these things add up to more time than I want to spend working. And I know it's a choice, so I'm satisfied that it's not perfect and it's not exactly as I would like it to be and I accept myself for not being as good at life as I would like and I laugh at it. Achieving balance is not a moment-by-moment process. It is a flow based on a foundation of well-being and self-care. Being mindful informs you of your process for self-care.

Nature teaches us a lot about balance. It works a cycle of seasons and within that cycle all sorts of disturbances crop up, such as storms and heat waves, which create glorious imbalances. Yet nature is perfect. If we accept that it is impossible to continuously balance it all, we can liberate ourselves to enjoy the uniqueness of each day.

## Auditing Your Work & Your Workplace

◆

*What is actually going on in your work life? Let's really drill down and find out what is affecting you. Later on we will assess what needs to change; but for now, let's identify the issues.*

Hopefully, having read this far you now have a greater perspective on what underlies unhappiness at work. Here are some questions for you to work through to identify the issues that affect you most:

- *Do I enjoy all of my work?*
- *Do I enjoy all the people I work with?*
- *Do I enjoy the system I work within?*
- *Do I like myself in this role?*

If you answered 'no' to any of these questions, examine yourself further, thus:

- *What niggles me about my work?*
- *What niggles me about the people?*
- *What niggles me about the system?*
- *What niggles me about myself in this role?*
- *What depresses me about my work?*
- *What depresses me about the people?*
- *What depresses me about the system?*
- *What depresses me about myself in this role?*
- *Of the above, what do I care about enough to take some action on or make different?*

## Trusting Emergence

Once you have skimmed through the questions, take some time to meditate on the answers. This is an exercise in trusting emergence. The result of this exercise is to end up with a clear sense of what it is you want to address. At this stage, I don't want you to know how to address it. *Allow* the uncertainty. Usually we fight uncertainty by jumping straight to a strategy; but when we learn how to allow uncertainty we get a ringside seat on what is happening that gives us much more data for informed decision-making.

Here are some examples of the result of this meditation.

### ANNA

Anna concluded that her work and colleagues were enjoyable but there were two tasks within her remit that relied on other people providing the information. If their information was incomplete, late or inaccurate, it impacted on her results. She recognized that a small systemic change could make a big difference to her stress and anxiety levels.

### ALI

Ali's meditation resulted in the realization that he fundamentally did not respect the managing director or believe in the particular niche product being offered. He knew that the evidence to support the product had been fabricated and the meditation raised his awareness of how much he was compromising for the sake of a salary. This meant that while he liked the industry and had high hopes for his progression in this job, it did not sit right with his own ethics and his truth was that he was compromising his own values.

## JULIE

Julie was very comfortable in her organization. She had been there a long time, was a trusted and senior member of the team, and had worked her way through virtually every role in the organization. The security was a good anchor. Lately, though, she had been unhappy and picking fault with things. After meditating, she realized that there was nothing wrong in the organization or her relationships with her colleagues, but she was yearning for more stimulation and challenge.

## DAVE

Dave was having trouble with a colleague. He experienced this colleague as abrupt and abrasive. This didn't sit well with his view of how colleagues should behave in a team. At first, he tried hard to ignore the problem and not allow it to get to him. After a while, he heard others complaining and found an outlet for his frustration by joining in conversations that maligned the colleague. Dave actually felt worse than he did before. Through meditating, he could see that the gossiping was not solving the problem, that the real problem was still there and needed to be addressed.

PETRA

Petra enjoyed helping people and her role gave her plenty of scope for doing so. She enjoyed interactions with the public. What she did not enjoy was the culture within the organization where discrimination against women and race were prevalent and although the systems gave the impression of providing equal opportunities, the discrimination was covert and subtle. She had already decided not to stay. Her struggle was the choice between walking away silently or publicly exposing the problems.

---◆---

'Life is one big road with lots of signs,

So when you riding through the ruts, don't you

complicate your mind:

Flee from hate, mischief and jealousy!

Don't bury your thoughts; put your vision to reality,

yeah!'

BOB MARLEY (1945–81)
SINGER-SONGWRITER

---◆---

## The Individual & the Culture

Now you should have a good idea of what it is you want to address and you should be able to tell if it is something you can address by changing your lens, position or perception – in which case you can initiate change from within yourself. Or it may be that addressing what you want to change involves asking others to change or do something different, in which case you will need to consider the culture of your workplace in order to work out how your invitation will be received.

Workplace culture is like a sea with everyone swimming in it. Whether you work in an office or a factory or remotely, you need to understand workplace culture and how it affects and influences everyone in it. Just like the sea, a strong current can affect everyone.

Official policies such as vision and mission statements will begin to give you an understanding of the values and foundations on which the organization is built. Other indicators are the structure and hierarchy. The line management and reporting systems and authority for decision-making are key contributors to the development of a culture. The intranet, newsletter, memos, meetings and social events all speak volumes about your workplace culture.

Every organization has its own personality and style that sets the tone for how decisions are made, how people get on with each other, how people dress, how they behave and how the organization progresses.

To identify the culture in your own workplace, consider the following questions:

- *What would you tell someone on their first day about how things are done?*
- *What would you tell a friend about where you work?*
- *Who is considered to be a star in the organization and why?*

- *Who is considered to be a troublemaker and why?*
- *What types of people thrive in the organization?*
- *What types of people fail in the organization?*

This is how a group of people get on and get things done. It's a set of norms that govern how everyone behaves. This affects how everyone meets challenges, recovers from setbacks, celebrates successes and mourns losses. It affects how and who advances within the organization. Having a clear understanding of the culture within your organization will help you make positive connections and get things done.

This culture is powerful because it influences how much you enjoy your work, your relationship with colleagues and your environment. It is the group personality and manifests as the best behaviour that a group of people can manage within the given set of conditions.

And of course there are subcultures where each team has developed its defensive or collaborative personality in relation to the whole. They are formed when recognition from co-workers meets needs better than that provided by the overall management.

### Fitting In

You might find that you have to adapt your ways in order to fit into the culture – and this is where unhappiness at work can stem from. If the culture suits you and fits in with your values, you won't have a problem. If you find your personal values at odds with the culture, you could find yourself compromising and feeling resentful. For example, if you believe that people should be allowed to get on with their work but the organization demands that you account for where you are every minute of the day, you will most likely find yourself in conflict with the organization. 'Fitting in' might mean doing things like dressing in a style that matches the culture or communicating in the style that is most prevalent or adopting a schedule that matches your co-workers'. The extent to which you can do this willingly will depend on the extent to which it conflicts with your own beliefs, attitudes and values. Telling yourself you should be able to 'fit in' when in actual fact you cannot or don't want to is one of the biggest sources of misery.

---

### Making a Point

A friend of mine worked as a designer. An industry standard at that time was that designers do not wear suits. However, in this company the managing director started to insist that the designers wear a suit when they went to meetings with clients. Their protests fell on deaf ears so they clubbed together and bought one suit, which they hung in the stationery cupboard and put on to attend client meetings. It didn't quite fit anyone and looked ridiculous. It didn't take long to revert to the culture of designers not wearing suits.

---

'If you believe that feeling bad or worrying long enough
will change a past or future event, then you are residing
on another planet with a different reality system.'

WILLIAM JAMES (1842–1910)
PSYCHOLOGIST & PHILOSOPHER

## Culture Change

While workplace culture is generally very static, that is not to
say it is not immune to change – so it's important to keep up.
A change in leadership or management structure, or an external
force such as a change in the market place, can result in
culture shifts. And culture change requires changed behaviour.
This can be a source of conflict if there are no conscious and
safe change processes in place.

Once you understand the culture, you can make choices
about what you buy into, what you will go along with, and at
what point you no longer wish to participate. This might change
your need to involve others or it
might highlight exactly who you
need to speak to. Understanding
this about yourself will help you
to feel more stable about what
you are choosing for yourself,
who you seek to involve, and
what your requests might be.

*Understanding
this about yourself
will help you to feel
more stable about what
you are choosing for
yourself…*

## REFLECTIONS

At this point, you should be in possession of an honest audit of your life at work. What does this mean? It just means being truly aware. A simple definition of awareness is 'noticing the fullness of life.' When you wake up, are you immediately immersed into the stresses, pressures and anxieties that surround you and invade you or do you wake up sensing the fullness of life that is beyond the limits of your created reality? Do you wake up to the vastness of the Universe and your part in it or do you wake up worrying about the minutiae? Can you close the distance between you and everyone else and find your connection to the whole? When you become aware, you are not fooled by your thoughts – you are aware of your motivations. You know when you are being honest with yourself and when you are hiding and you can communicate this with yourself. You are not fooled by your inner expert or your inner police officer. Instead you have a healthy relationship with your inner mediator. When you become aware, *nothing matters* and *everything matters* and you 'get' the paradox. Authenticity is the gift of awareness. Through conducting an honest audit, you will become authentic. By taking a long look at yourself and making an honest appraisal of your life at work, you can align with what is really important to you.

# CHAPTER FOUR

# THE
# CONFLICTS

*We all have personal power to escalate or
resolve a conflict. This chapter shares skills and
techniques to defuse petty conflicts and address
important ones. If you want to participate within
an organization, communication is essential. When
communication breaks down, people behave differently
to when communication is flowing. Understanding
how to resolve conflict is one of life's greatest skills
and the starting point is what is going on inside you.
Connecting with that is essential before attempting to
intervene in a conflict, because conflict with another
person is reflecting back to you a conflict
within yourself.*

## Connecting with Yourself

◆

*Before you can be of use to anyone in a conflict, you need to be in a compassionate state. This means to be aware of yourself, to have some cognition and comprehension of your own triggers and behaviours and to understand what is going on inside you.*

To do this you will need to find a practice that helps you to be in control of what, how and to whom you communicate. If you are fearful and stressed, you are less likely to contribute positively in a conflict. This is an interconnected process in which all the pieces need to be functioning simultaneously. It is not a linear sequence of consequences.

*Connecting with Yourself:* **FEAR**

Albert Ellis, founder of Rational Emotive Behaviour Therapy (REBT), suggested that there are three core beliefs with which humans disturb themselves:

**1.** The belief that we must perform outstandingly well at all times, under any set of conditions, and win the approval of others; and that failure to do so proves we are incompetent, unworthy and destined for failure, and therefore deserve to suffer. This is the state of being self-demanding.

**2.** The belief that any person with whom we have reason to be in any form of relationship must treat us decently, with consideration and fairness at all times. Failure to do so on their part means they are rotten, bad people who deserve to have a bad life and should be punished for being so despicable. This leads us to be demanding of others.

**3.** The belief that our life is impossible and not worth living if the conditions in which we live are not favourable to us. If it is not safe, hassle-free and quickly and easily enjoyable then we can't stand it and can't ever enjoy ourselves. This leads us to be demanding of the world.

When a conflict arises, it is easy to allow these beliefs to surface. Escalation of the conflict deepens our suspicion that the beliefs might be true and we become anxious that we will not be able to contain or cope with the associated feelings. The anxiety then manifests as stress so we plan our lives around avoiding actions that trigger feelings of stress – and this is where fear comes in. Without awareness of this inner process, we live in an energy of fear. Fear energy will hinder conflict resolution because the motivation for resolution is to save ourselves from our own feelings.

---

'If you have learned how to disagree without being disagreeable, then you have discovered the secret of getting along – whether it be business, family relations, or life itself.'

BERNARD MELTZER (1916–98)
US RADIO PRESENTER

---

> ### Defining Fear
>
> My definition of fear is the anticipation of negative and therefore uncomfortable feelings. If you approach a conflict from a place of fear, you are less likely to be able to resolve it. When trying to resolve conflict, you have to find ways to identify your stresses and put them to one side while you collaborate with the others involved to find a solution.

*Connecting with Yourself:* **TOXIC SHAME**

We experience toxic shame as the overwhelming sense that we are flawed and defective. Toxic shame puts you into a self-torment where you experience yourself as untrustworthy. It is self-generating. There is shame about the shame and because shame is so hard to admit to, it generates isolation and aloneness. We all carry some toxic shame because it is part of our social conditioning. It is the extent to which we choose to recognize and heal it that determines how it will affect us.

*Connecting with Yourself:* **STRESS**

When the pressure you feel exceeds your ability to cope, you will experience stress. This is the worry that if you cannot cope with the demands being made on you, your well-being is under threat. This problem arises from perceiving the strength of the demands to be greater than your ability to cope. The resulting stress behaviour is in response not to the stressor but to your perceived ability to cope. When we are stressed, we are less likely to contribute anything positive to the resolution of a conflict because the starting point in this state is a lack of sufficient personal resources.

## How Fear, Shame & Stress Determine Our Choices

Fear and shame manifest as anxiety and anxiety manifests as stress. The instinct to reduce stress drives us to make choices that are self-defeating.

Here's an example: John's manager asked him to write a report in time for a directors' meeting at the end of the week. John enthusiastically agreed to do it because he liked to say 'yes'; but halfway into the work he discovered that the amount of research involved could not be completed in the time so he could not meet the agreed deadline without a cost to the accuracy of the information. His self-demanding belief triggered feelings of fear and shame. He believed his manager would judge him as incompetent and his anxiety was related to the fear of how he would feel if she did and how it would increase his shame. The anxiety manifested as stress, which caused him to panic – and he ended up having a bad conversation with his manager. In that conversation he was defensive because protecting his own reputation was more important to him than the manager's needs. It's the sense of someone putting their own needs first that escalates the conflict.

Here's a rerun of that conversation:

MANAGER: *How is that project document going?*

JOHN: I'm not sure. I'm waiting on some information.

MANAGER: *What do you mean, 'I'm not sure'?*

JOHN: Well, I'm waiting on other people to give me answers and I can't be responsible for how long they take.

MANAGER: *Did you tell them you had a deadline?*

JOHN: Well yes, but this is a very tight deadline and some of the information takes longer to generate than the deadline.

MANAGER: *When did you know this?*

JOHN: It started to become apparent yesterday.

MANAGER: *So if I hadn't asked you about it this morning, when were you going to talk to me?*

JOHN: Well, I was trying to sort it out before coming to you.

MANAGER: *And what if you couldn't? I've put this project on the directors' agenda now.*

JOHN: Yes, I'm sorry I didn't anticipate this.

MANAGER: *Well, I want a solution by close of play today. The ball's in your court.*

JOHN: OK.

In this conversation, John's defensiveness gave his manager no confidence in him and led to a very unsatisfactory outcome where nothing good was decided. In fact, his manager preyed on John's lack of confidence because she stopped trusting that John would be capable of completing the task. The manager then went on to set him up to fail by isolating him to do the task without any assistance in order to prove John's incompetence. John, having been left to guess the best way forward, would inevitably end up producing something substandard in his manager's eyes. Here's how this conversation could have been handled if John was not connected to being self-demanding and was able to see that making mistakes is human and not the end of the world, and dealing with them openly and honestly will get a better result, not make him any less of a man.

JOHN: Can I have five minutes?

MANAGER: *Is it urgent?*

JOHN: It affects the document you want me to produce so I'm guessing you would want me to bring any queries to you as a matter of urgency.

MANAGER: *What is it?*

JOHN: When I agreed to do it, I hadn't given clear consideration to what was involved. Now I have, and I've discovered there are two bits of information I can't get accurate figures on by the deadline – so I want to alert you and find out what outcome would be best for your presentation at the directors' meeting.

MANAGER: *John, this is a bit of a pain, why didn't you know this when I asked you to do the job? I've put the project on the directors' agenda now and so I'm committed to do the presentation.*

JOHN: So you've put it on the agenda and it would be embarrassing to say we don't have anything ready? You don't want to take the blame for a mistake I made?

MANAGER: *Yes, I've worked hard to make sure this department has a good reputation and I don't want to damage it, especially when they are making redundancies.*

JOHN: So we need to pull together and give them something that shows you and the team in a good light?

MANAGER: *Yes.*

JOHN: Thank you for telling me that, it helps me understand the dilemma. In hindsight I can see that I could have been more attentive when I took it on and I can see this has created a hitch. How big a hitch is this to you?

MANAGER: *Well, in the grand scheme of things probably not that big, but you need to sort it out.*

JOHN: Yes, I'll take responsibility for sorting it but I need to know from you what would be acceptable given what we have to work with right now, and I'll take the rap on the knuckles after you have what you need. How does that sound?

MANAGER: *OK. Well, estimated figures will be fine – just asterisk them and explain in the appendix and be a bit more alert next time.*

JOHN: Yes, that will work for both of us. Thank you.

*Intention & Responsibility*

In this version of the conversation, John was proactive in supporting the manager to get what she needed. If you haven't experienced this way of communicating, it might be hard to believe – but I can hand on heart say that everyone accepts mistakes will be made.

Of course, when a mistake is presented, there may be an undesirable reaction. I make a lot of effort to get out of the habit of shouting when I'm presented with a mistake, which, culturally, I was brought up with. What people really have a problem with is the intention behind the mistake and how a person takes responsibility for a mistake. So if you have made a mistake and I am on the receiving end of it, the two things that count are:

*What Was Your Intention?*
Was this a genuine mistake on your part or were you consciously or unconsciously trying to cause loss, injury or harm to others? Did this mistake arise because you chose not to learn from a similar mistake you made in the past? Were you trying to protect yourself at a cost to me? Or are there some other factors that contributed?

*How Will You Take Responsibility?*
Are you genuinely doing everything in your power to make amends or are you consciously or unconsciously trying to sidestep your part in it? Are you willing to learn from the mistake and make the necessary changes? Are you willing to understand the impact of your mistake on the others involved?

*...when a mistake is presented,
there may be an undesirable reaction.*

## The Other Point of View

Now let's look at this issue the other way round. Someone else has made a mistake and their mistake has the potential to reflect badly on you. Let's look at the story from John's manager's point of view. Let's call her Jane. As a mediator, I was able to spend time with each of the parties to the dispute and hear their accounts of the situation separately. This is Jane's account of the situation.

Jane was aware that the directors were making cuts so she was looking out for ways to prove her own and her team's worth to the company. She was well aware of the politics of the company and proactivity was highly regarded. She knew a directors' meeting was coming up and wanted an opportunity to get in front of them and shine. She had an idea for a project but she knew an idea without evidence of its feasibility would be useless. She asked John to scope out the feasibility. She knew it was a tight deadline but not impossible and he agreed to take it on. Her biggest worry was that by putting herself in front of the directors she was also taking a risk of being in the firing line. Whether they liked the idea or not, they would ask testing questions and she wanted to be sure that all the information was in front of them. This was an exercise in being seen as an asset and she was doing it to save herself and her team from redundancy.

A couple of days before delivery, she asked John how he was doing. When he said he wasn't sure, she went in off the deep end. By the end of the conversation she was exasperated by his excuses and his uncertainty about whether he could do it or not, so she told him to sort it or else. On reflection it wasn't the best way to handle the conversation but her attitude was that, during these lean times in the company, anyone who couldn't keep up shouldn't be there and she couldn't afford to save people who weren't backing her one hundred per cent. So she would use this opportunity to see what John was really made of.

Now I'd like to re-script the conversation from the perspective of the manager working to get the best solution:

MANAGER: *How is that project document going?*

JOHN: I'm not sure. I'm waiting on some information.

MANAGER: *What do you mean, 'I'm not sure'?*

JOHN: Well, I'm waiting on other people to give me answers and I can't be responsible for how long they take.

MANAGER: *So, John, if I understand you correctly – you're waiting on some information and you're a bit anxious about how long it's taking?*

JOHN: Yes, I didn't appreciate when I took this on exactly what was involved.

MANAGER: *So it sounds as if you might have to consider what can be done in the time? Would you like us to take five minutes to discuss it? Would it help if I tell you what's important here?*

JOHN: Yes, I don't want to let you down or myself down but I got a bit stuck and was trying to figure it out for myself.

MANAGER: *How would it be if we talk about what went wrong later, but for now just deal with the immediate problem? I notice I'm feeling a bit impatient because I wasn't expecting this, so it would help me if we could just come up with a solution and get on with it.*

JOHN: OK.

MANAGER: *So, what's important is that I'm committed to doing this presentation at the directors' meeting and if they ask me awkward questions I want to feel I have the answers. So it's about reputation. What I need is the most accurate detail we can get. Tell me exactly what you do have, what is missing, and what you think we can do in the time.*

JOHN: I'm confident that the information is accurate with the exception of two costs – we don't know the transport costs and we don't know that because we don't know the weight and packaging for those items. If we guess the transport costs I could get them wrong by as much as fifty per cent but if you put it into the total project costs it only affects the total figure for the whole project by less than five per cent.

MANAGER: *So I could say in the presentation that the figures are accurate within five per cent? That's not so bad for an idea that's being proposed.*

JOHN: Phew, that's what I thought but I wasn't sure you would see it that way. I know you like detail.

MANAGER: *So if I understand you, part of why you didn't alert me is because you were worried about my reaction?*

JOHN: Yes.

MANAGER: *OK, that's enough for now, but I can see we should schedule a discussion about the way we're interacting.*

The point of these alternative dialogues is to show that anyone who is party to a conflict can change the outcome, whether they are the person making the mistake or the person who the mistake is impacting upon, and whether they are the manager or the report.

*In Conclusion*

In the dialogue examples between John and the manager, the conversation that took place was fear-based; John fearing that he could not complete the task and the manager fearing she would not get what she asked for. The conversation turned out badly. In the revised conversation, where John took the lead, he was confident for both of them and therefore there was a good outcome. In the conversation where the manager took the lead, she was confident for both of them and likewise got a good outcome.

You might think these are fantasy conversations that I made up. In fact, in my role as mediator I played the part of the manager for John, with Jane observing, and then played the part of John for Jane, with John observing. I did this openly so they could see what would happen if they entered the conversation from a different stance.

## Culture & Background

Whenever I am in Malta, where my parents are from, I feel completely at home with everyone shouting because it's normal. If you were to watch a Maltese current affairs programme, you would see that what generally happens is that within seconds of the first opinion being aired, everyone starts shouting at each other and the whole programme descends into a verbal war. From a different cultural perspective, it might look terrible – but Malta is a safe country with a good economy.

Understanding cultural reactions is really important, because if you interpret that reaction wrongly, the whole discussion can be meaningless or escalate over nothing. It's important to bear in mind that just because a person speaks the same language as you and works in the same company as you, they might not share the same cultural norms as you.

Each culture has its own rules about acceptable behaviour, which affect verbal and nonverbal communication. Making eye contact, being direct, observing personal space and physical contact vary in meaning from culture to culture. Display of emotion can be contentious between cultures. In some cultures, getting very emotional in a discussion is perfectly acceptable, while in others it is to be avoided at all costs. These differences can lead to communication problems.

## CONFLICT RESOLUTION

◆

*Resolving a dispute with finesse is a skill, especially when you are worried about your own and the other person's reactions; however, conflict resolution is very natural and, even though it sometimes seems counter-intuitive, we generally all prefer peace to conflict.*

THE CASE OF JOHN AND JANE demonstrates clearly that how you position yourself in a conversation determines the outcome. When I am mediating a workplace dispute, in the initial private meeting I ask the person about their willingness to resolve the dispute. Very often the response goes like this: 'Of course I am totally willing to sort this out, but you will never get them to sort it out.' At this stage I ask the person not to worry about the other person, but to concentrate on him- or herself. I say, 'Let's assume I have established the other person as willing to find a resolution with you, now tell me your willingness to do the same at a round table meeting.' Interestingly, most people are not scared of the other

◆

'Don't ever let them pull you down so low

as to hate them.'

BOOKER T. WASHINGTON (1856–1915)
BORN INTO SLAVERY & LATER AN ADVISOR
TO REPUBLICAN US PRESIDENTS

◆

## Values of Conflict Resolution

CONFLICT SHOULD BE OPENLY DISCUSSED

Conflict is a source of change for the better and a force for progress – if handled respectfully and openly.

CONFLICT IS A SHARED PROBLEM

By visualizing conflict as a shared problem, the parties can face it together and have the chance to build, rather than destroy, a relationship.

COOPERATIVE CONFLICT RESOLUTION DEPENDS ON SKILLS

People can be taught these skills to enable them to handle conflict more productively.

FORCE IS NOT AN APPROPRIATE WAY OF RESOLVING CONFLICT

Constructive conflict resolution requires trust and safety to settle differences.

THERE IS A NEED FOR SOCIALLY ACCEPTABLE ALTERNATIVES TO TRADITIONAL METHODS OF RESOLVING DISPUTES

For many involved in a dispute, the choices seem to be: ignore it, counter-argue, get revenge, call an authority, retaliate or use force. Mediation is an alternative to these. It costs less and takes less time. Unlike most other choices, mediation lets people reach agreement without deciding who is to blame, and without labelling someone a winner and someone a loser.

person's inability to resolve it. They are scared of how they will react to what the other person says. It's good to recognize that and, of course, one of the reasons for using a mediator is to help to keep the meeting calm and respectful.

If you don't have a mediator and you want to attempt to resolve a conflict for yourself or someone else, you have to learn how to relax in face of hearing things you don't like. If the way others behave induces stress, anxiety, fear or anger in you, you will need to learn how to step back. We do not make good decisions when we are stressed out or angry or fearful. Very often our next move escalates the problem. We make better decisions when we are relaxed and reflective.

## Learning to Relax

When stress takes hold, there will be three key changes in your state:

**1.** Physiological (*increased heart rate*)

**2.** Behavioural (*fight or flight*)

**3.** Subjective (*negative thoughts*)

The strength of these components varies, but most people will experience some physiological change, followed by a negative thought, which increases the physiological reaction, creating a vicious circle. One way of breaking this cycle is to focus on the physiological reactions and practise reducing your reactions, using a technique that induces relaxation. This is a skill that can be learned like any other skill – it takes time and practice but once you have learned it and mastered it, you will be able to call on it any time. In fact, it will become a natural part of how you are and that will mean less conflict and the presence to intervene in conflict with wisdom. The aim is to reach a point where you can relax 'on demand' and use it to counteract the physiological reactions you have to stressful situations. To achieve this, we're going to introduce a relaxation technique.

*Applying Relaxation*

The aim of this exercise is to teach yourself to relax by taking about ten to fifteen minutes each day to tense and release different muscle groups through the body in a sequence. You can do this seated comfortably. Work through the body in this order: feet, legs, hips, stomach, chest, back, shoulders, hands, arms, neck, face.

- Before you start, score how tense you are feeling right now on a scale of one to ten, with one being relaxed, five being normal and ten being totally tense. You will use this scoring again.
- Begin by breathing slow and evenly and then work through the sequence one muscle group at a time. Tense the muscles, hold for ten seconds, and release.
- Once you have worked through the whole body, sit and notice how this feels and re-score your level of tension on the one to ten scale.

- Once you feel you have mastered this by reducing your
  score on a consistent basis, reduce the exercise time to
  five minutes a day by skipping the tensing part. The idea
  is simply to work through the body and command the
  muscles to release into relaxation without tensing first.
  If you find any part of the body doesn't respond,
  tense the muscles there first. Keep on with the scoring.

Next you will begin to relate breathing to relaxing. This takes
time to practise but the idea is that you become aware of your
breathing and simultaneously relax the muscles in your body.
You are creating a cue for yourself:

NOTICE MY BREATHING: *inhale • exhale • relax*

You can practise this during everyday non-stressful situations
such as waiting at a bus stop or any other moment as you go
about your day-to-day. The more you can notice your breathing and use the cue to inhale, exhale, relax, the more it will
become second nature. Breathing will become synonymous
with relaxing.

In time you will be able to instruct yourself to RELAX on
command in non-stressful situations, until eventually you can
apply it in stressful situations. First you need to recognize
what you do at the onset of stress. How do you change? For
example, when I am experiencing stress I speak faster and
become more emphatic in what I am saying, so I'm learning
to notice what the triggers are for this so I can relax.

When you are relaxed, your participation with others will be more positive and confident. *In a conflict situation, setting aside your reactions and relaxing yourself is the single most important contribution you can make to the situation before you join in. The second most important contribution is to have equal consideration for the other person's needs as you have for your own.* Mastering that in a world where competition, external validation and deferring to rules are deemed to be important is quite a skill. Practising it in your own disputes is an even greater skill. In the organization I founded, the Centre for Peaceful Solutions, we still have situations where mediators find themselves in disputes and start to demonstrate disputant behaviour. Each event is another opportunity to learn.

## LISTENING & UNDERSTANDING

*How we engage with others involved in a conversation about change requires us to be sensitive to other people's feelings and needs and to really care about a quality of dialogue that can lead to a satisfactory outcome for everyone involved.*

CARL ROGERS WAS THE FOUNDER of the person-centred approach to therapy, which believes in a person's ability to make the right choices for themselves, regardless of the therapist's own beliefs. He suggested that parties to a conflict should sit together (or in a circle if there is a group) and *each person must restate the ideas and feelings of the previous speaker, accurately and to that speaker's satisfaction, before speaking up them-selves. Before presenting your point of view, you first have to achieve the previous speaker's frame of reference.* This means a conversational exchange that is focused on one person's point of view at a time. In John's dialogue earlier in the chapter, the first version had no single focus – both John and the manager were trying to defend their positions and were not listening to each other or trying to understand, so the manager simply used rank to 'win'. In reality, no one won. In the second version, John focused on the manager's needs first and by doing so got his own needs met without having to stress himself or the manager. The manager was able to treat him with respect because John was respecting himself. In the third version, the manager skilfully moved between John's needs and her own but did not confuse the two. In a workplace, a poverty con-sciousness often exists around time, which is seen as scarce – yet so much time is wasted on conflict without any real learning coming out of it.

## Doing Things in Order

It's really important to understand the flow of the journey in resolving a conflict. It's also important to recognize that when a conflict manifests as something everyone can see, it is likely that it had probably been brewing for some time. And it is helpful to understand that a conflict that has been brewing is

*Telling people to shake hands*
*and move on does not necessarily*
*resolve the problem.*

unlikely to resolve in one conversation – but the first conversation could be a turning point to rebuilding trust. Telling people to shake hands and move on does not necessarily resolve the problem. It hides it and the person, not having had the opportunity to learn from the situation, may simply move the problem somewhere else and choose another adversary, repeating the same pattern.

This is a logical sequence for the parties involved to follow once a conflict has surfaced:

ENGAGEMENT: The parties to the conflict need to have a good reason to want to resolve it. Having to work alongside each other and interdependency within the workplace are good reasons. Fear of getting fired is not such a good reason because it brings the person to the table in a defensive state.

MAKING ARRANGEMENTS: A time and place for discussion needs to be arranged. It is not helpful to ambush people. People need time to reflect and prepare.

PRE-MEETING: It's helpful to let everyone know what the issue is that is up for discussion and to identify the guidelines for the meeting – will someone facilitate the meeting and is that person trained or skilled in mediation or facilitation; is it confidential; will notes be taken; how long is the meeting; is the room private; who else will be there; what is the aim. If you have a facilitator, it is helpful to allow each person some private time in advance to vent about the issue and get some acknowledgement for how they feel.

MEETING: The meeting should have a structure, such as introductions followed by each person having uninterrupted time to speak, followed by flip-charting the issues that arise from each speaker. The issues should be sorted into an order and discussed one at a time with the purpose of arriving at a solution that helps everyone. If there is no facilitator, responsibilities for things like time keeping, note taking, and ensuring everyone has an equal voice should be distributed between participants to avoid one person being perceived to be in control. Proposals for settling the matter should be explored and objections discussed until an agreement is reached. Agreements should be doable, measurable and time limited. A follow up meeting should be agreed.

REVIEW: This will look at whether the agreements have been kept, or what went wrong if they didn't work and how that can be rectified. In an organization, there would also be a clear policy on what resources will be put into the matter and at what point the organization will protect itself by taking a different route to resolution.

---

### Communication Blockers

The following is not helpful in resolving conflict:

ORDERING  *'You must…'*

THREATENING  *'You had better…'; 'If you don't…'*

PREACHING  *'You should…', 'When I did your job, I used to…'*

LECTURING  *'Here is where you're wrong…'*

JUDGING  *'You don't care about this job.'*

EXCUSING  *'Don't worry, it'll get better.'*

ANALYSING  *'You need to admit to yourself you have a problem.'*

PROVOKING  *'She said you were rude to her.'*

INTERROGATING  *'What were you doing? Who else was there? How long for?'*

MORALIZING  *'This is not how we behave in this company.'*

---

*Engagement*

To be successful, you will be continuously gaining and retaining engagement with others. Remember, you have to be relaxed to be able to do this. If you cannot relax, find some help. This process can be used between two colleagues or for a group. If it doesn't work or the issues are too complex, you will need a mediator. A trained and experienced mediator will have the expertise to manage all the people involved and the complexities of the situation.

Here's a simple example of getting engagement:

**A**  *May I have two minutes of your time?*

**B**  Why?

**A**  *Before I go into that, I want to be sure you can give me two minutes. If this isn't a good time, I can come back.*

**B**  Go ahead.

**A**  *I want to address a problem I'm having in a way that works for both of us. I think we have a problem communicating; I'd like us to have a brief chat about it. Would you be willing to help me find a way for us to get on better?*

**B**  OK.

**A**  *What would suit you?*

**B**  Not now. Later.

**A**  *What about 5pm in the meeting room if I book it?*

**B**  OK.

**A**  *I would like us to discuss how we can communicate better and I'd like it to be confidential between us with no one else there, just to see if we can work it out. Is that OK for you?*

**B**  And if we can't work it out?

**A**  *We'll both have to think about it but I will agree not to do anything about it without talking to you first.*

**B**  OK.

Can you identify the ways in which that dialogue created engagement?

Here's another version with A as an intermediary:

**A** *May I have two minutes of your time?*

**B** Why?

**A** *Before I go into that, I want to be sure you can give me two minutes. If this isn't a good time, I can come back.*

**B** Go ahead.

**A** *I want to check something out with you. It's my understanding that C and you are not communicating well. I wondered if that was affecting you at all?*

**B** I don't have a problem with it. I've got better things to worry about.

**A** *So if I understand, you don't have a problem with it?*

**B** That's right. So why are you here? What has C said?

**A** *You're interested in what C has said?*

**B** Yes.

**A** *C believes there is something to sort out and I came here to find out your willingness to help.*

**B** Like I said, I don't have a problem.

**A** *Yes, I am clear that you don't have a problem. I'm making a slightly different request. I'm wondering if you would be willing to help C, who is struggling with this?*

**B** Sure. What do I have to do?

**A** *Thank you, that's very cooperative. You don't have to do anything you don't want. I'm trying to arrange an informal, private meeting, which I'd like you to attend. Would you be willing to do that?*

**B** OK.

Can you identify the ways in which the intermediary got engagement?

Try to break down the various dialogues in this chapter and see if you can understand what is going on. The key point is that there is a shift in position that seeks to build collaboration and allows the other person to choose what happens next.

Doing this is only authentic if you genuinely care. It will not work as a tool of manipulation. If you have a premeditated outcome in mind and you are trying to manoeuvre the other person, the process will break down because doing that starts from a lack of trust in others.

---

## REFLECTIONS

In this chapter we got down to practical steps in resolving conflict and looked at how what we say and how we say it affects the outcome of a conversation. I hope you have seen how connecting with yourself is the first step and that once you have become mindful and relaxed you can begin to look at the conflict in the context of the other people involved. It is my hope that what you take away from this chapter is that, like any other problem in life, it is helpful to have a proper process in place and not to expect that a problem can be undone in less time than it took to create it.

# CHAPTER FIVE

---

# TURNING WORK INTO PRODUCTIVE PLAY

*To realize change and increase joy, you
need a plan. And the plan itself should be a
happy experience, not a gruelling punishment.
You will consider the choices you have made and
how they affect you today and then work through the
choices you can make today to change the course of
your future. This chapter is all about how you want
work to be for you and how you will get there through
a structured and reflexive learning process.*

# The Plan

◆

*This is the fun bit, where you really invest in yourself and learn what makes you tick. You're going to set aside two weeks to get into a revealing dialogue with yourself and I want you to find the most enjoyable way you can of doing it.*

So far this book has been like a patchwork quilt. You have been quietly collecting all the different pieces of material. During the collection process you looked at each piece that you found or was given to you and made a decision as to whether to save it or discard it. These pieces could be suggestions you've seen in the book, reflections on your work up to now, or emotional responses from the exercises. Hopefully, when you looked at each piece you were mindful of its qualities. You gave some thought to whether it would fit into the overall design and whether you liked it. Now we're going to sort through all the pieces you saved and find a way to put them together to make something you really like and enjoy over the course of the rest of the book. Of course, it will probably be a fiddly job and you might have to unpick some bits and start again, and you might change your mind about other bits – but it's important that you enjoy this process.

The place to begin is to recognize that you are doing something for *you*. You are investing in your own happiness. What I want you to avoid is doing something you don't enjoy for some future-focused prize. So I'm setting out a framework for a two-week plan and I want you to experiment with the tasks and find the enjoyment in them. If you can't find any sense of enjoyment, don't do it. Find another way to achieve the outcome. Design your own two-week plan by picking out what appeals and adding more tasks that you like. During the two weeks you will practise mindfulness, open intuition, allow your creative self to emerge and find some direction.

If you are reading through the book for the first time, you can begin preparing for your two weeks in your mind's eye. If you are rereading the book, having completed all the exercises and reflected on the contents over the twelve weeks I initially suggested, you can now choose your start date, allowing some preparation time, which I describe later. Decide on a two-week period when you are in your normal routine with nothing unusual happening. For example, don't try this if there is an important family celebration coming up, or you are about to have your appraisal at work, as these events evoke different emotions, which may confuse the results.

---

'Nothing is work unless you'd rather be
doing something else.'

GEORGE HALAS (1895–1983)
PIONEER IN AMERICAN FOOTBALL
& OWNER OF THE CHICAGO BEARS

---

## Pre-Plan

In the lead-up to your two weeks, plan as you would for a holiday by making sure everything is in place. Have you got in enough of your usual food supplies? Are your usual childcare arrangements properly in place? Are there bills that need paying? Have you paid the parking fine? These are examples of things that can put you under pressure if you leave them until the last minute. If you normally rely on your partner or someone else to take care of some or all of that stuff, explain to them that you need a two-week period of no unusual disturbance. Ask them to anticipate anything they might need and get their support for this period. If you experience any problems with this pre-process, choose a new start date rather than forcing it to happen on a particular date. If you really can't get the start date organized in a simple and trouble-free way because there are endless obstacles, work on the relaxation technique (see pages 101–4) until you reach a calm state – and remember that we invoke everything that happens. We aren't always conscious that the decisions we've made have led to our current situation. It's only when we reflect on this – how we've resisted change and denied the problem at various stages in life – that we realize this is the case.

It is the paradox between our desire to control the external and our refusal to accept ourselves as authors of our own lives that creates much of the human suffering we inflict on ourselves and others.

## Friends

Once you have decided upon a starting date, choose a group of trusted friends. A couple of days before you start the two-week process, tell them you are undertaking an exercise in mindfulness to help you decide your work for the future and ask if they would be willing to stand by you in that process. Tell them that it doesn't involve a huge amount of their time but that there is a specific task you would like them to do. The wording is written below. Copy this out onto a pretty post-card and give it to them as an invitation.

---

### Invitation to Friends

*Dear [add name]*

Thank you for agreeing to stand by me for the next two weeks. It would help me if you follow this exactly. Once a day for two weeks, starting on [add date], I would like you to call me into your mind and imagine me surrounded by light and feeling really happy. It doesn't matter if it is just for a second or longer but it will really help me if you do it every day and then let me know you have done so. You can send me a text, instant message, email or just call me to say 'I thought of you today surrounded by light and feeling happy'.

Thank you.

*[Your name]*

---

## UNDERSTANDING RITUAL

◆

*Rituals can help us to prepare and get us in the right frame of mind.*
*A ritual is anything we mindfully repeat before or after a task. Rit-*
*uals exist in everyday life whether we are conscious of them or not.*
*For example, every morning I drink a cup of tea soon after waking.*
*That is a ritual. In this section we're going to explore rituals and*
*find some to suit you.*

WHEN I WAS TRAINING TO BECOME A REIKI MASTER, I developed a meditation practice to prepare for getting into the desired state. I would enter the room, close the door, light a candle, light some incense, put on some gentle music and stand with my hands in prayer position and ask for quiet and calm. At the end of the meditation, I would blow out the candle, extinguish the incense, turn off the music and stand with my hands in prayer position and give thanks for all that is. This was my ritual for getting into the zone and leaving it. I performed this ritual without fail until I no longer needed it and I could self-command myself into the required zone. Before I see a client, I scan the room, tidy up the cushions, bring in water and turn my phone to silent. There are practical reasons for doing these things but the timing of those actions is also ritualistic. It creates a partition between what I was doing beforehand and what I am about to do. It helps me to be mindful.

**CLEAR THINKING**

If you regularly use alcohol or recreational drugs to escape from your inner feelings, you need to consider whether you are ready for this two-week plan because it requires you to think clearly. Dependency on stimulants and depressants is a different subject, which I don't cover in this book.

The two-week plan involves a set of rituals and tasks that you will slot into your daily routine. I'd like you to invent a few of your own. It could be as simple as stroking the cat for two minutes before leaving for work. The idea is that it slows you down, creates a partition between tasks and brings you into the present. At the World Spiritual University in London, calming music is played for about two minutes every hour and all conversations and tasks stop as everyone lapses into silence, becoming present and mindful. This 'pause' is just long enough to remember what is and isn't important, so during this two-week period you will be using rituals as reminders to 'come back to your senses'.

### Writing It Down

Keep a pen and pad handy to jot things down every morning and then from time to time during the day if it helps you. Processing goes through many stages. There is a difference between thinking it, saying it out loud and writing it down. Each one of those stages shapes the thought and feeling, so it's good to jot things down as you go.

## All Set

Now everything is in place. You have made preparations; devised some rituals; you have a pen and pad to hand and friends standing by you. Are you enjoying this? Take stock of the process so far and before you start, ask yourself these questions: What is your mood? What did you enjoy? What didn't you enjoy? Do you still want to do this? It is voluntary. You don't have to do it. You can back out. You can tell your friends you've changed your mind. You can make any choice you want. What choice are you making now? Is it for enjoyable reasons?

If there is any sense of non-enjoyment, please examine this before you start the two-week plan. If you feel good to proceed, read on. If not, read the section on non-enjoyment. In any case, read the plan through ahead of time so you can position the tasks in your schedule and enjoy the anticipation of doing them and investing in your biggest asset – you.

*Take stock of the process*
*so far and before you start,*
*ask yourself these questions…*

## NON-ENJOYMENT

I have no definitive answer for why you don't find enjoyment in some aspects of your life but if you don't, then I suggest you start to examine what blocks you from enjoyment. Enjoyment is a choice that depends on how you view circumstances, events, yourself and others. Here are a few reflections.

Has non-enjoyment become a habit or your default position? Do you require the world to show you something first by giving you a sign or laying a path for you before you will engage and before you allow the experience of enjoyment?

Has disappointment got the better of you? Do you often feel let down because you had higher expectations than how it turned out? Does that get in the way of your enjoyment?

Do you not care very much for yourself? Do you dislike yourself? Do you worry about your motivations and intentions? Does that prevent you from enjoying your life?

Are you worried about the future and how your life will turn out? Do you worry about personal or financial security? Is the future hindering the present?

If any of this resonates with your non-enjoyment of your life and you would like to find more joy, then the only answer is change. What you change and how you change is your choice – but it starts inside you.

## YOUR TWO WEEKS

◆

*This is the format that each day should follow. If you start work at a fixed time each day, consider how much earlier you will need to leave for work in order to get there without any stress in the morning. Consider how much sleep you will need and work out your waking and sleeping times accordingly.*

**WAKING TIME** When you wake and before you get out of bed, write whatever comes out of you. Without thought or planning, just transfer everything that comes out onto the paper. No censorship, just a stream of consciousness before you become engulfed in your day. You should allow about fifteen minutes and write something each day, even if all you can start with is 'I don't know what to write'.

**PREPARING FOR THE DAY** Follow your usual routine for that particular day of the week but imagine it is happening in slow motion. Imagine you are standing beside yourself watching yourself do whatever it is you do, be it showering, eating breakfast, walking the dog, getting the kids ready or checking emails. Check in with yourself as to why you are doing the task at all or in that particular way? What purpose does it serve? Is it enjoyable? Could it be more enjoyable? Then smile with yourself. Follow this example. Tell yourself, 'Oh, look, I'm making the bed because I like to find it tidy when I get back in the evening, so I'm investing in myself by giving this time right now' – then smile about it and continue. Or tell yourself, 'Oh look, I'm making the bed when I don't really want to, it doesn't matter if it's a mess, I don't need to do this' – then smile about it and make a choice about whether to make it or do something different.

**WHEN PREPARATIONS ARE COMPLETE** Add in a ritual like stroking the cat or lighting a candle or doing a handstand, whatever works for you. Then make a declaration to yourself about how you want to conduct yourself this day. For example; 'Today, I am calm and have time to speak with compassion to anyone who approaches me'; or 'Today, I am focusing on the completion of tasks'. It would be really helpful to jot it down in your notepad.

**NOW GET ON WITH THE DAY** Travel, work and do tasks as usual, but set an alarm to go off once an hour so you can step out of what you are doing for two minutes. Is this really difficult? Do you work intensively with others in a way that prevents you from having that much autonomy over your time? Then work around it and be creative. What do you do when you need the bathroom? Can you withdraw for a few minutes? Can you schedule the hour breaks differently to suit natural breaks in your work cycle? It has to be easy to do and enjoyable to find a way. That's the key. These are not rules, they are guidance, and it has to suit you – so find a way that works for you. Depending on where you are, try one of the following for your two minute break:

- Gently shake out your hands
- If you have been focused on a computer screen, look as far away as possible
- Stretch your face muscles
- Give yourself a quick scalp massage
- Run on the spot very gently
- Have a stretch

Now ask yourself about the last hour. Have you enjoyed it? Are you enjoying right now?

**AFTER WORK** Between the end of work and whatever you do next, use a ritual to create a partition – anything from sitting down in silence on your own to doing a jig. If you can engage some colleagues in it, that's even better. A couple of years ago, the charity I run was renting business premises where the landlord happened to leave behind a grand piano, which we agreed to take care of. As luck would have it, one of our team was a pianist and I like to sing, so we devised a group ritual called 'song for the day'. We would each have a turn at choosing a song to express the mood of the day and then we would sing it. Whatever you choose as your partitioning activity, make it something that allows you to close down your work mode and acknowledge your labour. Remember that work does not necessarily mean being an employee in an organization. Even on so-called rest days we often do some work such as cooking or cleaning or paying the bills. Creating partitions applies to all of these things.

**BETWEEN WORK & SLEEP** Carry on with whatever you normally do and be really kind to yourself. Be aware of your inner dialogue and only say compassionate things to yourself. So if you find yourself going over something that happened during the day or remonstrating with yourself over something in a way that sounds like you are telling yourself off or blaming yourself, stop and talk to yourself like a very kindly and wise old aunt who has your best interests at heart. Things she might say to you include:

- 'Have a good night's sleep and think about it in the morning when you are less tired.'
- 'You were doing the best you could in the circumstances and with what you knew at the time.'
- 'This can all be sorted out and you don't have to worry about it in your leisure time.'
- 'You've done enough for today.'

During the course of the day, you should have received messages from friends who are standing by you. Remember to send them a thank you. If you didn't receive a message from any one friend, make a choice. Talk to them about it and be prepared to understand what happened or ignore it and carry on without resentment; but in any case stay focused on yourself and don't be distracted by this.

**BEFORE GOING TO BED** Check back to your declaration for the day and ask yourself how well it worked. Take a minute to celebrate what went well and mourn what didn't. Go over what could have been better and replay it as if you had all the time and resources to make it turn out well. This is visualization. Create the imagery so that it is realistic and you believe you are really doing it. To make the visualization work, you need to make it very vivid in your imagination and break the action down into small components while also sensing the feelings and ending with a positive result. This part of your two-week plan is essential because you will learn from doing it and it's where you can begin the process of exchanging old habits for new ones. If you can't imagine yourself doing it, then you probably won't do it.

**JUST BEFORE SLEEPING** Close your eyes and consider how you breathe. Work towards evenness in the inhalation and exhalation and slow your breathing down by taking slightly longer on each breath, maintaining a rhythm that is entirely comfortable. Focus on the inhaling and exhaling. Place your hands on any area of your body that is comforting and allow yourself to 'be' until you relax and ultimately fall asleep.

## Review

At the end of the two weeks, start to sift through and review the information you have gathered about yourself and your situation. Socrates commented that the unexamined life is not worth living. Where you are is the sum of all the experiences and choices you made up to this moment. The last two weeks have been an exercise in awakening to how you do things. It's time to recognize any detrimental choices and be OK with it because everyone makes mistakes. Evaluate how happy you are at work. Look into what areas there are for improvement and what you would like more of in your life. No life is going to be trouble-free. There will always be obstacles. It is not realistic to strive towards being obstacle-free. It is realistic to learn how to change your reactions to obstacles so that you can be at peace. Compassionate change that is planned and mindful is healthy. Aggressive change that harms and injures is unhealthy. Reflect on your strengths and your weaknesses.

**1.** *What have you learned about your life at work?*

**2.** *What do you want to change?*


## The Crossroads

After all this information gathering, you will want some direction, and this next exercise is about finding it. It might be that you now know what you want. It might be that you have found that you really are content with the way things are; or it might be that you have discovered just how intolerable your work life is and you want to take immediate action.

You will need one large piece of paper and some A4 sheets and a marker pen, a small space to move around in, and your notepad and pen. On the large piece of paper, draw a circle large enough for you to stand in. Place it on the floor. On the A4 sheets of paper, write down different outcomes. Write as many as there are options, somewhere between five and ten.

Here are some examples, but write ones that apply to you.

- Do nothing and wait
- Get another job
- Talk to my boss
- Get affairs in order before making change
- Do some networking
- Take a radical step

Place them all around the circle. Now copy that configuration onto your pad.

Stand in the circle, then inhale, exhale and relax. Turn around slowly, scanning each of the options. Notice any rises or falls in your energy levels. Step out of the circle and move onto any one of the options. Assess your *positive* energy for this option using a scale of one to ten, with one being the lowest. Try not to dwell on it too much. If you have followed the other exercises in this book and become aware, your first answer will be your most intuitive. Write down the score for that option on your pad. Repeat this with all the options. At the end of the exercise, prioritize the options by their scores.

---

'It's impossible,' said pride.

'It's risky,' said experience.

'It's pointless,' said reason.

'Give it a try,' whispered the heart.

ANON

---

You can break down this exercise even more by placing the highest scoring option inside the circle, placing around the circle new choices that would support that option, and repeating the process. So if your high score was 'Do nothing and wait', you could put a series of waiting periods on the pieces of paper, ranging from one week to one year, and continue with the scoring process until you have an answer that resonates for you. If your high score was 'Take a radical step', you could place a series of options ranging from 'Resign my job' to 'Ask for a raise' around the inner circle and repeat the scoring process. This exercise will show you what actions you have the most energy for and enable you to set your direction.

---

## REFLECTIONS

The outcome of this journey should be for you to understand what work means to you – whether you are enjoying your work in its current form, or have adjustments and changes you would like to make. You have a direction and a set of supporting tasks. It's now a case of beginning. No one can do this for you. It's up to you when you start. Just remember that every action you take has a consequence, so the closer you are to taking that action from a calm and relaxed place, the more likely you are to have a harmonious outcome.

# CHAPTER SIX

# HARVESTING YOUR EFFORTS

*Mindful practices will help you achieve your plan and form a sound platform for ongoing fulfilment. If you have worked your way through this book and want to harvest what you have invested in, then think about how to begin. We all start things in different ways — some of us need to dip our toe in the water a few times and others go for immersion. It's how you support yourself and have care for yourself and others that matters. In this chapter I offer you ways to support yourself to continue on the path of mindfulness at work.*

## WAKE UP

◆

*We spend a lot of time in a state of numbness where we bury our feelings. Sometimes it's important to do that. If I'm very busy, I choose to put my feelings to one side and plough through my work. But that is always temporary. When it becomes your habitual state, you are no longer alive.*

FEELING IS THE DIFFERENCE BETWEEN being alive and dead. Mindfulness is about recognizing this 'autopilot' state of numbness and stepping out of it to deliberately become aware of your mental and emotional habits and make a choice in the present moment. Ways to spot that you are operating on autopilot include:

- Feeling depressed about knowing exactly where your career will be in ten years time or not being in the job you imagined you would be doing by now.

- Never pausing for a break in your career or not having tried anything new in a while and feeling it's too late to do it now.

If you recognize this state, go back to the beginning of the book and engage with the 'feelings' and 'needs' exercises (see pages 32–7). The more you can adjust your thinking into sensing your feelings and needs, the better equipped you will become at finding strategies to meet your needs rather than strategies that just fend off feelings.

'Never too old, never too bad, never too late,

never too sick to start from scratch once again.'

BIKRAM CHOUDHURY
YOGA GURU & FOUNDER OF BIKRAM YOGA

## Open Your Intuition

Analytic thinking is often necessary to navigate our way through the world of work and analysis is vital to decision-making in business under the mainstream economic models we use; but it becomes unhealthy when we allow analytic thinking to override intuition. If you have become super-analytical, you will need to remind your intellect to include your intuitive feelings in its assessment of what is right for you. Intuition is knowing without words. Learning to use your intuition will help you find the joyful path to your goals because your intuition leads you to aliveness. Intuition does not require explanation – it just *is*, and you know when it resonates. Following your intuition can make your work effortless because it increases the flow of 'chi', or life force. Where there is greater life force, there is abundance and prosperity. Where there is abundance and prosperity, there is happiness and success. This is the universal law of attraction. This appears to have nothing to do with money, but money too is an energy and will in turn be attracted to the energy of abundance and prosperity.

## Support

No one can operate well in isolation, so if you are planning on making changes, it is especially important to find support. Talking is a simple and effective way of giving and receiving support. Sometimes it might be prudent to use a professional – for example, if there is a particular problem you want to address with an expert or you would rather pay for a safe and confidential space – but in any case, it is really important to have a support network in place. When I was a 'business-woman', I had a friend who had risen to a director's role in her workplace. We created a hotline to each other, where we could pick up the phone in those moments of complete frustration and have a good cry or rant to get it out of our system. We reciprocated for each other and never referred to it at any other time. From where I am now, it feels a bit primitive – but at the time it was a real help.

It's also important to think about where you are currently getting support and whether that is working for you. Standing around the water cooler complaining about colleagues is really a tragic request for support. 'Tragic' is a word used in nonviolent communication to mean 'ill-fated'. If you can identify these requests for support as tragic, you can begin to find better ways to get care.

Another great thing to do is to support others. Giving support can be very rewarding. Passing on and sharing your own wisdom can be helpful.

## Giving & Receiving Support

It's useful to agree expectations for your support sessions. Without such a framework, conflicts and resentments can arise if, for example, one party feels the level of support is not what they hoped for or the other feels that liberties are being taken; and the very process of discussing the framework increases authenticity and rapport.

**WHAT DOES CONFIDENTIALITY MEAN?** Confidentiality may mean never discussing or referring to the content or the conversation under any circumstances. In other circumstances you might want to frame what you are willing to keep confidential – for example, I wouldn't keep confidential anything that was asking me to collude against another person, so I would state this up front.

**HOW MUCH TIME AND HOW OFTEN?** It's important to know what time you are giving or expecting to receive. Are you expecting to be able to call unannounced or should there be some notice, such as an advance text? Should time be limited or is it open-ended? Is it a regular slot or just when initiated by one of you?

**WHAT HAPPENS IN A CRISIS OR EMERGENCY?** Can you reach each other day or night or is there a limit to when and how? What constitutes an emergency to each of you?

**WHAT SUPPORT IS NEEDED OR WANTED?** Is it a listening ear with no feedback or is this a session to help plan a way forward or is the supporter's professional expertise useful?

**HOW WILL YOU REVIEW AND EVALUATE THE USEFULNESS OF THE SUPPORT?** Is a simple expression of gratitude enough or do you want to analyse what has been achieved periodically?

**WHAT'S THE PROCEDURE IF ONE OF YOU WANTS TO STOP?** Is it OK just to say 'thanks, I don't need this any more' or 'I don't want to do this any more', or is a longer closure process needed? Ending is a responsibility to ensure that each person gets proper closure.

**HOW WILL YOU MANAGE IF A CONFLICT ARISES?** Are you comfortable with total honesty or do you agree to take it to mediation? It's important for you to fully understand what will happen if you find yourself in a disagreement, because this is not a good time to try and figure out what happens next as you will probably have different views.

## MINDFULNESS IN ORGANIZATIONS

*One immediate step you can take is to introduce Mindfulness Practice to your workplace – as Gandhi said, 'Be the change you want to see in the world.' If you have found this book useful, the chances are your colleagues will too; and if your colleagues find it useful, the chances are the organization will too.*

THE UNIVERSITY OF WISCONSIN conducted a randomized, controlled study of the effects on brain and immune function of an eight-week clinical training programme in mindfulness meditation applied in a work environment with healthy employees. Twenty-five subjects were tested concurrently with a non-meditating group. Brain electrical activity measured before and immediately after each session, and again four months after the end of the meditation course, suggested that mindfulness training leads to brain changes consistent with enhanced immune function and effective handling of stress and that these changes were present for at least four months.

Contemporary research is beginning to prove what mindfulness practitioners have known for centuries. Paying attention, having awareness, finding acceptance and developing compassion helps us to be more flexible and adaptive, which reduces stress and helps to free us from suffering while simultaneously building positive health and well-being. At a time when businesses are being called on to go beyond doing just what is legal by considering what is ethical, what sensible organization would not want to help its biggest asset, the people, to find ways to be healthy and able to work with joy and willingness?

A mindful organization will set out to achieve greater congruence between its intentions and its actions. However, often the delivery falls short of the original plan – for example, if the directors' vision is to have 95 per cent happy staff and happy customers, it might achieve 95 per cent happy customers but find it only achieves 70 per cent happy staff.

That constitutes a gap between intention and action. Rather than reviewing an action after the event, congruence requires us to view an action in real time. This means considering the way we work together and the way work gets done to achieve an alignment of actions with outcomes. Doing this means shedding the robust armour that fends off feelings and, instead, deliberately developing sensitivity to early warning signs of discord, wherever it might appear within the business, and having the tools and processes to work quickly towards resolution. It means allowing people to enquire about any aspect of the business without fear of reprisal so they can get meaning and purpose for their tasks. Doing these things helps people to function in the face of adversity and grows the group capacity to act as a team.

When an organization designs mindfulness into its overall strategy, the leaders can let go of having to be 'on top' all the time (which is unsustainable for any human being), because when the individuals grow as a team and are knowledgeable of their organization's aims, they will naturally start to act for the organization's goals and thus require less leadership. Using collaborative tools for dialogue and expertise sharing through the use of mediation and facilitation leads to happier teams, who will work as much for their team goals as their individual goals because they have a bigger stake in their working environment.

## Start a Mindfulness Meditation Group at Work

Set a start date with a time and place – choose a time when as many people as possible can join in and find a place where you will not be disturbed. If you are lucky, your workplace might provide a space; if not, then find somewhere. Then send out emails to your network. This wording might work:

- Would you like to improve your health and well-being?
- Would you like to become more resilient to everyday stresses?
- Join our new weekly Mindfulness Meditation Group. [*Insert date, time, place*]
- Invest thirty minutes of your time.
- All welcome.
- Bring a cushion.

Ask people to bring cushions unless there are some already at the venue. Meditate at the scheduled time, even if you are alone. Remember you are starting this group to meditate – so meditate. If you start, others will join at some point. Put on some calming instrumental music on a low volume. Organize the twenty minutes. Here's a suggestion:

- Arrival and sitting in circle in silence.
- Start with a quick go around – for example, name and how you're feeling.
- You might take it in turns to prepare a short text of about two hundred words to hand out, on a subject such as awareness, compassion, acceptance or empathy.

- Now meditate. Everyone should take it in turns to lead the meditation by saying:

  *'First close your eyes and focus on the way you are before the impulse arises to judge, fix or censor anything. Now slowly take a few deep breaths. Steady your body into a position that will be comfortable for the next twenty minutes. Scan your body for tension and release. And just sit. If your mind wanders, just allow the thought to pass through and come back gently, breath by breath.'*

- After the allotted time (I suggested thirty minutes for the whole session, allowing five minutes for beginning, five minutes for coming round and twenty minutes for meditating, but you might want to allow more or less time), the person leading the meditation should bring everyone out of it by saying:

  *'Now just focus on your breathing and slowly open your eyes and come back into the room.'*

- This final point is extremely important. Do not overrun on time. When people go into meditation they need to trust that they will be called back to the present at the pre-arranged time, because being late might impact another part of their life.

You could keep a sign-in sheet to create a group and send out notices of future sessions. If your meditation group takes off, you will have evidence of attendance and you may be able to get the organization to take it on board. Give yourself permission to make this happen.

## In Closure

The purpose of this book is to find ways to make work more enjoyable.

For her book *The Top Five Regrets of the Dying*, Bronnie Ware worked with dying patients and asked them about their regrets. High up the list was 'I wish I hadn't worked so hard'. If work isn't productive play, you will wish you hadn't worked so much because you didn't enjoy it – and we pretty much always wish we could have found another way to achieve the same goal when we haven't enjoyed ourselves.

Sometimes, circumstances will reduce or change your options, but you always have the power to choose how you react and respond to whatever is in front of you.

I hope this book has awakened a spirit of creativity and ingenuity in you – because from that place, anything is possible.

# INDEX

## ACKNOWLEDGEMENTS

❖

*I'd like express gratitude to all the people
I learned from whilst remembering that some lessons
have been easier to learn than others. As ever, my children Sam
and Rosy feature high up in my motivation to have contributed
something worthwhile to society. And Rosy's recent marriage to
Sa'ad, which crosses continents and cultures, gives me more
reasons to be mindful of what a wonderful world it is.*